The Renaissance

James A. Corrick
AR B.L.: 10.3 Alt.: 1516
Points: 5.0   UG

The Renaissance

Other titles in the World History Series

WORLD HISTORY

The Renaissance

James A. Corrick

LUCENT BOOKS
A part of Gale, Cengage Learning

GALE
CENGAGE Learning

Detroit • New York • San Francisco • New Haven, Conn • Waterville, Maine • London

For more information, contact
Lucent Books
27500 Drake Rd.
Farmington Hills, MI 48331-3535
Or you can visit our Internet site at gale.cengage.com

LIBRARY OF CONGRESS CATALOGING-IN-PUBLICATION DATA

Corrick, James A.
     The Renaissance / by James A. Corrick.
        p. cm. — (World history series)
     Includes bibliographical references and index.
     ISBN 1-59018-836-5 (hard cover : alk. paper) 1. Renaissance—Juvenile literature.
I. Title. II. Series.
     CB361.C67 2006
     940.2'1—dc22

                                                                          2006010109

Printed in the United States of America
  4 5 6 7 12 11 10 09 08

Contents

Foreword

Each year, on the first day of school, nearly every history teacher faces the task of explaining why his or her students should study history. Many reasons have been given. One is that lessons exist in the past from which contemporary society can benefit and learn. Another is that exploration of the past allows us to see the origins of our customs, ideas, and institutions. Concepts such as democracy, ethnic conflict, or even things as trivial as fashion or mores, have historical roots.

Reasons such as these impress few students, however. If anything, these explanations seem remote and dull to young minds. Yet history is anything but dull. And therein lies what is perhaps the most compelling reason for studying history: History is filled with great stories. The classic themes of literature and drama—love and sacrifice, hatred and revenge, injustice and betrayal, adversity and overcoming adversity—fill the pages of history books, feeding the imagination as well as any of the great works of fiction do.

The story of the Children's Crusade, for example, is one of the most tragic in history. In 1212 Crusader fever hit Europe. A call went out from the pope that all good Christians should journey to Jerusalem to drive out the hated Muslims and return the city to Christian control. Heeding the call, thousands of children made the journey. Parents bravely allowed many children to go, and entire communities were inspired by the faith of these small Crusaders. Unfortunately, many boarded ships captained by slave traders, who enthusiastically sold the children into slavery as soon as they arrived at their destination. Thousands died from disease, exposure, and starvation on the long march across Europe to the Mediterranean Sea. Others perished at sea.

Another story, from a modern and more familiar place, offers a soul-wrenching view of personal humiliation but also the ability to rise above it. Hatsuye Egami was one of 110,000 Japanese Americans sent to internment camps during World War II. "Since yesterday we Japanese have ceased to be human beings," he wrote in his diary. "We are numbers. We are no longer Egamis, but the number 23324. A tag with that number is on every trunk, suitcase and bag. Tags, also, on our breasts." Despite such dehumanizing treatment, most internees worked hard to control their bitterness. They created workable communities inside the camps and demonstrated again and again their loyalty as Americans.

These are but two of the many stories from history that can be found in the pages of the Lucent Books World History series. All World History titles rely on sound research and verifiable evidence, and all give students a clear sense of time, place, and chronology through maps and timelines as well as text.

All titles include a wide range of authoritative perspectives that demonstrate the complexity of historical interpretation and sharpen the reader's critical thinking skills. Formally documented quotations and annotated bibliographies enable students to locate and evaluate sources, often instantaneously via the Internet, and serve as valuable tools for further research and debate.

Finally, Lucent's World History titles present rousing good stories, featuring vivid primary source quotations drawn from unique, sometimes obscure sources such as diaries, public records, and contemporary chronicles. In this way, the voices of participants and witnesses as well as important biographers and historians bring the study of history to life. As we are caught up in the lives of others, we are reminded that we too are characters in the ongoing human saga, and we are better prepared for our own roles.

ca. 1300
The Apache and Navajo settle in what is now Arizona and New Mexico.

ca. 1325
The Aztec found Tenochtitlán (Mexico City).

1368
The Ming dynasty comes to power in China.

ca. 1400
The Inca begin building an empire in South America.

1300	1325	1350	1375	1400	1425	1450

ca. 1307
Dante begins writing the *Divine Comedy.*

1405
Zheng He leads a Chinese expedition that establishes trade by sea with India, Africa, and Arabia.

ca. 1450
Johannes Gutenberg builds his printing press.

the Renaissance

1474
Construction begins on the Great Wall of China.

ca. 1520
In India, Nānak founds Sikhism, which combines elements of Islam and Hinduism.

1521
Hernán Cortés conquers the Aztec.

1512
Persia (Iran) adopts Shiism as its state religion.

1608
The telescope is invented.

| 1475 | 1500 | 1525 | 1550 | 1575 | 1600 | 1625 |

1492
Christopher Columbus reaches the Americas.

1543
Nicolaus Copernicus's *On the Revolutions of Heavenly Spheres* is published.

1591
Moroccan troops capture the trade city of Timbuktu and end the Songhai Empire in Africa.

1508
Michelangelo begins work on the ceiling of the Sistine Chapel.

1517
Martin Luther draws up his Ninety-five Theses.

1600
Edo (Tokyo) becomes the capital of Japan.

Leaving the Middle Ages

The Renaissance was one of the great cultural movements of history. Beginning in Italy in the 1300s, it spread rapidly throughout much of Europe during the next three hundred years. These were centuries filled with dramatic change and achievement in many areas, among them economics, politics, art, and science. Many of these accomplishments laid the foundation of current Western civilization.

The Roots of the Renaissance

The people of the Renaissance saw their dynamic culture as a sign that they lived in an age completely divorced from the previous thousand years—the Middle Ages. They saw the Middle Ages as a time of chaos and ignorance that separated the Renaissance from the ancient world of Greece and Rome. That ancient world had ended with the collapse of the Roman Empire in the late fifth century.

For those living in the Renaissance, their age was linked not with the Middle Ages but with the world of ancient Greece and Rome. They believed that only the ancients had reached the same level of achievement. Indeed, the Renaissance saw itself as a revival or rebirth of the old Greek and Roman culture, and from this idea of a classical revival came the very name *Renaissance*, French for "Rebirth."

In reality, many of the roots of the Renaissance were in the Middle Ages. Interest in ancient Greece and Rome came from medieval students and scholars who had discovered Arabic translations of classical works in Muslim-controlled Spain and brought them north. Even some important inventions were medieval in origin. The magnetic compass that directed Renaissance explorers to Asia and the Americas was developed in the twelfth century.

The Forces of Change

It was, in fact, this medieval society that stood on the brink of the Renaissance in 1300, but it was a society in turmoil. As the historian Charles G. Nauert comments:

> Medieval civilization contained some fundamental defects.... The crisis that became evident in the fourteenth century has even been compared to the crisis that shattered [ancient] Roman society in the fourth century and led ultimately to Rome's fall. Unlike Rome, European civilization survived only because it was flexible enough to make fundamental modifications.[1]

Feudalism, the medieval social order, no longer worked. It had developed at a time when most of Europe was farm-based and political power rested in the hands of the local nobility. However, late medieval society was more complex, and feudalism was inadequate to meet the demands of this new era. Among other things, it had no provisions for dealing with the towns and cities that had grown up during the last centuries of the Middle Ages. Nor did its loose

This fourteenth-century manuscript illumination depicts a class at Italy's University of Bologna. A new thirst for knowledge propelled the Middle Ages into the Renaissance.

political structure provide the means to build and run countries with strong central governments, which were beginning to take shape in England and France.

The Catholic Church had also provided stability to medieval society. However, the late medieval church was suffering from its own problems. Many of the clergy had used their position to build political power and personal fortunes. The pope had fallen under the control of the king of France and would not be free of this influence until the last quarter of the fourteenth century. Because of these and

Renaissance Europe

— Boundary of the Holy Roman Empire

NORWAY

SWEDEN

SCOTLAND

North Sea

DENMARK

IRELAND

WALES

ENGLAND

London

Atlantic Ocean

Paris

FRANCE

HOLY ROMAN EMPIRE

MILAN

VENICE

GENOA

FERRARA

PAPAL STATES

Rome

FLORENCE

NAPLES

PORTUGAL

SPAIN

other problems, the church had become a disruptive social element rather than a healing one.

Other forces were also at work altering the medieval way of life. European economy was changing because of an increase in trade, which had begun with the Crusades, holy wars aimed at freeing the Middle East from Muslim control. Returning crusaders had introduced Europe to spices, silks, and other luxuries found in the Middle East. The growing trade sparked interest in other parts of the world, and what had once been a closed society began to open up and expand.

Responding to Change and Opportunity

The transformation of the Middle Ages into the Renaissance came about because the people of Europe developed new ways of doing things. And in so doing, the Renaissance crackled with energy and activity. Trade and industry were booming. Explorers were establishing sea routes to distant Asia and reaching new lands in the Americas. Scholars were founding libraries and filling them with unearthed ancient manuscripts. They were also writing new books, many detailing recent scientific discoveries in such fields as astronomy and anatomy. Artists and sculptors were producing great works in paint and stone.

Thus, to Europeans this time of the Renaissance was a new age filled with awesome accomplishments. Many would have agreed with the French physician Jean Fernel, who wrote in the early 1500s, "The world sailed round, the largest of Earth's continents discovered, the printing press sowing knowledge, gunpowder revolutionizing the art of war, ancient manuscripts rescued and the restoration of scholarship, all witness to the triumph of our New Age."[2]

The many accomplishments of the society were also mirrored in the varied interests and achievements of specific individuals. For instance, the anonymous biographer of the fifteenth-century Italian Leon Battista Alberti says that Alberti, who thought of himself as an architect, also "taught himself music, and his work gained the approval of skilled musicians. He took up civil law for some years. At the age of twenty-four he turned to physics and mathematics."[3] Others, such as Leonardo da Vinci, would be as versatile, giving rise to the term *Renaissance man*.

In science, art, government, and finance, creativity dominated the Renaissance. For, as the scholar Robert Ergang writes, "the age of the Renaissance is one of the great creative periods of history. Few historical eras have displayed greater intellectual and artistic vitality. The Renaissance period was, above all, a time which gave new direction to intellectual endeavor by turning the thoughts and strivings of people into paths leading to what is now called modern civilization."[4]

Chapter One

The New Learning

The Renaissance was marked by a renewed interest in ancient Greek and Roman works. As a consequence, the fourteenth and fifteenth centuries saw one of the greatest scavenger hunts in history. All over Europe eager searchers ransacked the dusty shelves of monasteries and old public buildings. Stashed away in these places were treasures—not gold or silver but ancient Greek and Roman manuscripts. As a result of this search, the surviving writings of such classical authors as Plato, Sophocles, Cicero, and Plutarch came into Renaissance hands. The searchers, financed by princes, merchants, and other rich folk, did their work well, and by 1500 they had unearthed almost all the ancient writing that had survived the Middle Ages.

The powerful and wealthy collectors of these manuscripts built libraries to house their growing collections, and these libraries drew those interested in learning as much as possible about the people,

ideas, and art of antiquity. Out of this study came the philosophy known as humanism, whose rapid spread throughout western Europe was aided by several factors, including new technology, a rise in literacy, and sponsorship by wealthy folk. Humanism was destined to become central to much of Renaissance culture.

The Birth of Classical Study

The passion for antiquity appeared first in fourteenth-century Italy. Here, scholars were surrounded by the ruins of the Roman Empire and thus became fascinated with Italy's ancient past. To understand that past better, they turned to surviving Roman writings.

Among the first of these Italian scholars was Francesco Petrarca, better known as Petrarch, an enthusiastic and untiring collector and promoter of classical literature. Born in 1304, he was supported by a series of wealthy sponsors, or patrons, and thus was able to devote his life to studying and writing about antiquity. Historian Crane Brinton writes that before Petrarch's death in 1374

> he assembled a splendid private library and found in an Italian cathedral some dusty and forgotten letters of [Roman statesman] Cicero which threw new light on that Roman's political career. Petrarch so admired the past that he addressed a series of affectionate letters to Cicero and other old masters and composed a Latin epic in the manner of the *Aeneid*.[5]

Rediscovering the Ancient Greeks

Petrarch and other Italian scholars were equally enthusiastic about ancient Greek culture. Their interest was sparked in part by admiring references in Roman manuscripts to Greek writers, such as Homer, Plato, and Sophocles, whose work had long since been lost to western Europe. In part, Petrarch and others shared the medieval reverence for the ancient Greek philosopher Aristotle, whose writings had reentered western Europe during the Middle Ages as Latin translations of Arabic editions found in Muslim-controlled Spain.

Beginning in the fourteenth century, many missing Greek works were brought to Italy by refugees from the crumbling Byzantine Empire. Centered on the Balkan peninsula, the Byzantine Empire was descended from the eastern portion of the old Roman Empire, and its libraries contained many original Greek manuscripts. In the fourteenth century the Ottoman Turks began conquering the Byzantine state, completing the task in 1453 with the capture of the imperial capital Constantinople.

Many Byzantines sought safety from the Turks in the west. Armed with copies of

Renaissance scholar Francesco Petrarca—better known as Petrarch—was an untiring and enthusiastic collector and promoter of classical literature.

ancient Greek writings, these refugees set themselves up as teachers. As the scholar Will Durant observes, they "served as carriers of the classic germ: so year by year Italy rediscovered Greece."[6]

Few of the early Italian scholars, however, mastered the Greek language. According to Brinton, Petrarch "never learned Greek well enough to read it, although he could at least gaze reverently at his manuscripts of Homer and Plato."[7] The problem with Greek was that with rare exceptions, the language had not been spoken or written in the west for centuries. Not until the close of the fourteenth century did large numbers of western Europeans begin to learn the language.

Improving Latin

Even after Greek reappeared in the West, Renaissance Europeans often preferred to read ancient Greek works in Latin translations. Reading Latin posed no serious problems because it had been used throughout western Europe during the Middle Ages by the Catholic Church and by medieval scholars.

Indeed, early Renaissance scholars believed that they knew Latin as well as had the ancient Romans. To their surprise, however, they noticed while studying Roman manuscripts that differences existed between ancient and medieval Latin, and they began to view the medieval version as a corrupt form of the language. Many purists demanded a return to the eloquence they believed only classical Latin possessed. In 1444 Lorenzo Valla argued for a rigid adherence to the rules of ancient Latin

in his *Elegantiarum linguae Latinae* (*The Elegances of the Latin Language*). Valla's work proved to be very popular with many scholars, and the *Elegantiarum linguae Latinae* helped to create a whole corps of intellectuals, whose chief goal was to work out the rules for classical Latin grammar. A few scholars, however, were offended by Valla's insistence that the Latin of Cicero, whose writing was much admired, was grammatically flawed.

Valla's book also found readers outside scholarly circles. Many middle-class merchants, for instance, could read Latin since it was considered necessary for communicating with foreign businesses and were thus interested in improving their use of the language.

Humanism

The study of Latin, Greek, and classical works was initially labeled the New Learning, but in time it became known as humanism because its practitioners were concerned first and foremost with human affairs, as opposed to the spiritual or divine. Humanist scholars saw humans as superior to nature. They further believed that humans had free will—that is, each individual was responsible for his or her actions. Consequently, to the humanists the search for truth and goodness was a personal matter.

Despite humanism's focus on the human individual, its followers did not deny the existence of God, nor did they see any conflict between humanism and religion. Indeed, many leading Renaissance humanists belonged to the clergy. To the

The Latin Legacy

In The Elegance of the Latin Language *(1444) Italian humanist Lorenzo Valla argues that Latin is the most important legacy of ancient Rome.*

When I consider for myself the deeds of our ancestors [the Romans] and the acts of other kings and peoples, ours seem to me to have excelled all others not only in empire but even in the propagation of their language. No people has spread its language so far as ours has done.

The Roman dominion, the peoples and nations long ago threw off as an unwelcome burden; the language of Rome they have thought sweeter than any nectar, more splendid than any silk, more precious than any gold or gems, and they have embraced it as if it were a god sent from Paradise. Great, therefore, is the power of the Latin language, truly great in its divinity, which has been preserved these many centuries.

Who does not know that when the Latin language flourishes, all studies and disciplines thrive, as they are ruined when it perishes? For whom have been the most profound philosophers, the best orators, and finally the greatest writers but those indeed who have been most zealous in speaking well [in Latin]?

Donald R. Kelley, *Renaissance Humanism.* Boston: Twayne, 1991.

humanists, God was a given from which, according to historian Ernst Breisach, "they proceeded to investigate man, his capacities, his deeds, and his accomplishments."[8]

Humanism and the Printed Word

During the fifteenth century humanism spread beyond Italy to the rest of western Europe. Its spread was aided by an important new technology: the printing press. Until the Renaissance, books were produced by hand, each copy being individually written out. Then, around 1450, the printing press was invented in Germany, with many historians giving the credit to Johannes Gutenberg.

Although printing technology had been developed in China as early as the second century A.D., the mechanism was a clumsy affair of hand-carved wooden letters, which generally produced poor-quality prints. However, the fifteenth-century printing press was combined with another innovation, movable metal type (perhaps another Gutenberg invention). This combination turned out pages with sharp, clear letters.

Even though books could now be more easily produced and distributed, early printed volumes were large, bulky, and

The spread of knowledge during the Renaissance was possible because of the invention of the printing press. History has credited Johannes Gutenberg (inset) as its inventor.

expensive, affordable only to wealthy individuals. By the end of the fifteenth century, though, the introduction of smaller type made for smaller, inexpensive books. Suddenly books, some in pocket-size editions that people could carry around with them, became available to everyone, significantly speeding up the spread of classical knowledge and humanistic ideas.

The Rise of Literacy

Another significant factor helping the spread of humanism was an increase in literacy. Unlike the Middle Ages, during which only the clergy and a few others could read, the Renaissance saw readers from all social classes and walks of life. They included, of course, scholars and students but also aristocrats, merchants, and tradespeople. They numbered among them both men and women. Indeed, by the mid–sixteenth century about half the population of London could read and write to some degree; other European cities had similar literacy rates.

The printing press, by making books plentiful and easily affordable, certainly led more people to reading and writing.

However, even before the advent of the press, literacy was on the rise in Europe. The aristocracy saw literacy as a civilizing influence, and those who could read and write generally advanced further in political careers. The middle class found literacy a valuable tool in running a business, which required written records and reports. Beginning in the late fifteenth century, guilds, or professional trade organizations, required that their members be able to read and write.

The Spread of Education

This desire and need for reading and writing prompted the growth of schools. Elementary schools popped up all over Europe, attended by both boys and girls. These schools taught reading, writing, arithmetic, history, geography, and religion. Boys could receive at secondary schools and universities advanced education, which included Latin, philosophy, and law. Girls were occasionally instructed in these subjects by private tutors.

Formal schooling was mostly confined to the middle class. The nobility generally taught their children at home, whereas the poor—laborers and peasants—often did not go to school at all because they could not afford the fees. However, they sometimes attended charity schools run by the church.

Patrons and the Medici

The spread of humanism throughout Europe was further aided by wealthy patrons. In the northern Italian city-state of Milan, for instance, the ruling Visconti and Sforza families were enthusiastic humanists, supporting many teachers, artists, philosophers, and scholars. The Visconti were Petrarch's patrons for a time, and the Sforza sponsored Constantine Lascaris, who, in 1476, produced the first book in Greek published in Renaissance Italy.

However, it was farther south, in Florence, that humanism found its most zealous patrons, the Medici. Perhaps the richest family in Renaissance Italy, the Medici earned their money as successful bankers and traders. Their wealth eventually bought them political control of Florence, which they turned into one of the great cultural centers of the Renaissance.

Cosimo de' Medici, who ruled Florence from 1434 to 1464, for example, established the first public library in Italy, supported numerous artists and writers, and encouraged the study of Greek. Cosimo's library, its door open free of charge to teachers and students, was filled with thousands of ancient manuscripts. Many of these works were originals, scavenged by Medici agents from Greece and Egypt, often at great cost to Cosimo. The remainder were copies made by a permanent staff of forty-five scribes, again supported by Medici money.

Cosimo's powerful grandson Lorenzo, the tyrant of Florence from 1469 to 1492, was an even more generous patron than his grandfather. Known as "the Magnificent," Lorenzo was himself a scholar, schooled in both philosophy and Greek. He expanded his grandfather's manuscript collection, once saying that he wished he could spend his entire fortune on the purchase of books. He also took an active part in the debates of the humanists with whom he surrounded himself. Of Lorenzo's passion for knowledge, the fifteenth-century Italian political writer Niccolò Machiavelli writes:

He loved exceedingly all who excelled in the arts, and he showered favors on the learned. To give the youth of Florence an opportunity of studying letters he founded a college at Pisa [then under Florentine control], to which he had appointed the most excellent professors that Italy could produce. In his conversation he was ready and eloquent. There had never died in Florence—nor yet in Italy—one who left behind him so wide a reputation for wisdom.[9]

The Platonic Academy

In 1439 Cosimo de' Medici organized and financed the Platonic Academy, which promoted study of the classics. Under Lorenzo, the academy became one of the most important intellectual centers in Italy. Similar humanist clubs would spring up all over Italy, and many played important roles in the development of Renaissance thought, art, and science.

These Renaissance associations were modeled on the ancient Greek philosopher

Lorenzo de' Medici sits surrounded by his artists. The flowering of Renaissance humanism was largely due to the patronage of wealthy families like the Medici.

Praise for Cicero

Renaissance scholars much admired the Roman statesman Cicero, whose writing served as a model for period authors. Here, writing in 1345, Petrarch explains the reasons for this admiration.

Allow me to say, O Cicero, that you lived as a man, you spoke as an orator, you wrote as a philosopher. I applaud your talent and your eloquence, O great father of Roman elegance, not I alone but all who bedeck themselves with the flowers of Latin speech are grateful to you; for it is with the waters from your wellsprings that we irrigate our fields, frankly admitting that we are sustained by your leadership, aided by your judgments, and enlightened by your radiance. In a word, under your auspices, so to speak, we have achieved whatever writing skills and principles that we possess.

Petrarch, *Letters on Familiar Matters.* Vol. 3. Trans. Aldo S. Bernardo. Baltimore: Johns Hopkins University Press, 1985.

Plato's Academy, in which teachers and students met to discuss and debate philosophical issues, such as the nature of knowledge, love, and death. Plato was a revered figure during the Renaissance, his popular appeal based on his belief that values—or, as he called them, ideas—were absolute and unchanging. Plato's belief in absolute ideas fit nicely with Christian theology, particularly his insistence that all earthly things were created and given shape by the highest of these ideas, which Plato labeled "the Supreme Form of the Good." The fifteenth-century humanist Marsilio Ficino describes the Good as the "one wise intelligence in command, the leader of all things, which can give a beginning to everything and establish an end."[10] It was an easy step for Christians to conclude that this Good was God.

Florence's Platonic Academy saw as its special mission the squaring of Platonic thought, as well as classical philosophy in general, with Christianity. The academy was not the first to be interested in this matter. Petrarch, in the previous century, had sought to create a stronger brand of Christianity by wedding the teachings of the church with the philosophy of Cicero.

The Humanists of Florence

A number of famous humanists were members of the Platonic Academy. Marsilio Ficino, who became the head of the academy, produced a 1483 Latin translation of Plato's work that helped popularize the Greek philosopher throughout Renaissance Europe and remained in print through the next century. Angelo Ambrogini, better known as Politian, was an early expert on Greek writers, and his Latin translation of the *Iliad* made Homer's work available to those who did not read Greek.

Ficino's nephew, Giovanni Pico della Mirandola, was perhaps the most accomplished of all the group's members, fluent not only in Latin and Greek but also in Hebrew and Arabic. Reading widely in works written in all these languages, he sought a common factor that would unite all religions, ancient and modern. Although he failed to find that factor, he did establish the disciplines of comparative religion and comparative philosophy.

In 1486, in an attempt to find his common religious denominator, Pico della Mirandola proposed nine hundred theses, or questions, for a debate to be held in Rome. Pico della Mirandola even promised to pay the way of anyone who was interested in taking part but was too poor to travel. However, the debate never took place because the pope at the time, Innocent VIII, ruled that some of the theses smacked of heresy, opinions contrary to the church's teachings. Pico della Mirandola defended himself against this charge in his *Oratio de hominis dignitate* (*Oration on the Dignity of Man*, 1489), which many historians see as the manifesto of humanism. In the *Oratio* Pico della Mirandola defends the human focus of humanism when he says, "I have read in Arabian books that nothing in the world can be found that is more worthy of admiration than man."[11]

The Prince of Humanists

Toward the end of the fifteenth century humanism began to spread beyond Italy to the rest of Europe. Indeed, the most famous of all humanists was a northern European, Desiderius Erasmus. Born in about 1469 in the Netherlands, Erasmus became known as the prince of humanists because he dominated the intellectual world of his day until his death in 1536.

Erasmus's early education owed little to humanism as the Italian Renaissance had yet to influence northern European thinking to any great extent. In 1487 he became a monk, but he left the monastery after a few years to study theology in Paris. Bored and uninspired by his course work, he began tutoring other students and reading classical literature.

Then, in 1499, at the age of thirty, Erasmus followed one of his pupils to England and there met an English humanist, John Colet of Oxford. Colet so inspired Erasmus that the Dutch monk plunged into a study of Greek so as to turn himself into a humanist scholar.

Within a few years Erasmus had achieved his goal, and over the next thirty years, he taught and lived all over western Europe. He wrote thousands of letters to other important people of his day and turned out major humanist works, such as the satirical *Encomium Moriae* (*Praise of Folly*, 1511). In this work Erasmus uses humor to ridicule the failings, or follies, of nonhumanists and the world they have constructed.

Erasmus was one of the first best-selling European writers. His work appealed to the growing reading public of the time, and the printing press made his work available to these readers. The *Praise of Folly*, for instance, became an instant best

Dutch humanist scholar Desiderius Erasmus dominated the intellectual world of the Renaissance.

seller, going through forty-two editions of one thousand copies each during the author's lifetime. Only the Bible sold more copies.

Humanism in the Universities

Almost as important as Erasmus to the promotion of humanism was another northern European, the Frenchman Guil-

laume Budé. Recognized as one of the leading scholars of his day, Budé wrote important books on Roman law and the study of the Greek language. In the latter, his 1529 *Commentarii linguae Graecae* (*Commentaries on the Greek Language*), he conveys his deep enthusiasm for a language that he did not even learn to read until he was twenty-six (supposedly he was so absorbed in his Greek studies that he forgot his own wedding).

Like other humanists, Budé was a firm believer in the importance of an education strong in the classics, and he thus became involved in educational reform at the university level. In 1530, while serving as court librarian for the French king Francis I, Budé helped establish one of the first humanist universities, the College of France.

Unlike older European universities, such as the French Sorbonne or the British Oxford, lectures at the College of France were given not just in Latin but also in Greek and Hebrew, and courses covered a wider range of classical learning. Students in other Renaissance universities followed the medieval practice of taking only those classes relevant to their chosen area of study. This professional, specialized education prepared a student to be a priest, a doctor, or a lawyer.

Humanists, such as Budé, rejected this tightly focused university education. Instead, influenced by the ideas of Cicero, they favored a more general, wide-ranging education that would expose the student to a large variety of human experience through a thorough reading of both Greek and Roman literature. The humanists felt that such a general education would develop all of a student's capabilities. Also, it was Budé's belief that, when combined with Christian teaching, a general classical education built character because it exposed students to many examples of heroic and moral behavior described by the ancients.

Through teaching and writing, humanists such as Budé and Erasmus influenced the development of the Renaissance. As scholar John Hale points out:

> By the early sixteenth century the influence of classical scholarship, and its popularization through translations and paraphrases, had acquired a critical mass which produced unstoppable chain reactions. There was hardly a branch of inquiry, from jurisprudence [law] to mathematics, military science, and the arts, that was unaltered by the stimulus of a relevant text, artifact, or record of historical experience. [12]

Not least of the things touched and changed by humanism was the practice of religion.

Chapter Two

Religious Reform

The Renaissance was a period of religious turmoil, as reformers sought to purify the Catholic Church and its clergy. Many of those calling for reform were northern humanists, such as Erasmus. Although many church critics wanted to correct the church from within, others, most notably Martin Luther, found more radical solutions. These latter reformers broke with the church and initiated the Protestant Reformation. In response, the Catholic Church launched the Counter-Reformation.

The Worldly Church

Those who sought to reform the Catholic Church believed that the institution had become too worldly and no longer served the spiritual needs of its members. They pointed out that many priests were illiterate and poorly trained and, consequently, were all too often unfit to minister to their congregations. High-ranking church officials, bishops and even the pope himself, were attacked as being more interested in secular politics than in church matters. And indeed, Renaissance bishops often were deeply involved in local and national politics, some holding important government posts.

The popes of the time often acted more like secular rulers than spiritual leaders. For instance, Alexander VI, pope from 1492 to 1503, accused in his time of being a devil and a monster, assisted the political ambitions of his illegitimate son, Cesare Borgia, by diverting church money for Borgia's use. Alexander also helped the French invade northern Italy in exchange for Borgia's being named a duke by the French king. Alexander's successor, Julius II, who was pope from 1503 to 1513, put on armor and led Vatican armies on a number of campaigns, conquering several of Rome's neighbors. Such acts led the Italian historian Francesco Guicciardini to write of the popes in his 1561 *Storia d'Italia* (*History of Italy*):

Having obtained temporal [worldly] power by these methods, they gradually forgot divine commands and the salvation of their souls. . . . Their aim was no longer a holy life; no longer the spread of Christianity; no longer doing good to their neighbor. They became interested in armies, in wars against Christians, the accumulation of treasure, new laws, new methods to draw money from every side. [13]

Bishops and Sinners

Church critics were also upset by two common money-raising practices of the Renaissance popes: simony and the selling of indulgences. Simony was the sale of high church offices, those held by bishops, to wealthy individuals, most of whom had no theological training. Further, most lived far from the regions they administered and rarely, if ever, visited these areas, many choosing rather to live in Rome. Known as unsuitable bishops, these office holders' sole concern was the collecting of church taxes that all church members were required to pay. Each unsuitable bishop kept a large percentage for himself and passed the remainder to the papacy.

The other papal instrument, the indulgence, was a way for individuals to buy penance for their sins. As Brinton writes:

The theory of indulgences concerned the remission of the punishment of sins. Normally, the repentant sinner has to undergo punishment on earth in the form of penance and after death in purgatory, where sinners repentant on earth atone by temporary but painful punishment for their sins and are prepared for heaven. Indulgences could remit penance and part or all of the punishment in purgatory. [14]

Thus, instead of having to undergo some form of penance, such as hours of prayer or performing acts of charity, a buyer of an indulgence could pay a fee and escape the necessity of such acts. Further, people could buy indulgences against future sins or to help dead relatives gain an early release from purgatory.

Christian Humanism

Although calls to end simony and indulgences, along with other forms of church corruption, were heard in southern Europe, it was the northern humanists who took the lead in this campaign. This aspect of northern humanism came to be called Christian humanism. As Charles G. Nauert observes, "*Christian humanism* is often applied to describe that part of the Northern Humanist movement that made reform of the Church the principal focus." [15]

Among the most vocal of the northern humanists was Erasmus. In several key sections of the *Praise of Folly*, the Dutch humanist ridicules the excesses and weaknesses of the clergy. In 1504 Erasmus wrote in his *Enchiridion militis christiani* (*Handbook of the Christian Soldier*) that the Catholic Church needed to return to the simplicity of the early church and to follow more closely the teachings of the early Christian leaders. As a humanist he felt that the search for religious enlightenment was a personal affair and that the clergy should therefore exercise little authority in such a matter.

Martin Luther

It was, however, another, the German Christian humanist Martin Luther, who

Renaissance church leaders like this bishop often bought the position for money.

became the point man for church reform. Born in 1483 and ordained in 1507, Luther was particularly angered by the sale of indulgences. In November 1517 Luther, then a professor of theology at the University of Wittenberg, directly challenged church authority. He drew up his Ninety-five Theses, which argued that the pope had no power to remit punishment for sin and thus that the sale of indulgences was a cheat.

Over the next few years Luther went much further in his quest for reform. He came to believe that the only source of God's word was the Bible and that all the writings and pronouncements of the church, even those from the pope, meant nothing.

Luther also became convinced that salvation rested only in faith. Traditionally, the church claimed that salvation was a combination of faith and good works, such as acts of charity. Lutheranism, as Luther's teachings came to be called, was the seed from which the Protestant Reformation sprang.

The Spread of Lutheranism

In 1521, in an attempt to stamp out Luther's heresy, Pope Leo X excommunicated the German reformer—that is, expelled him from the church. The pope hoped that the threat of excommunication would frighten others from embracing Lutheranism. Such was not to be the case, for many Germans agreed with Luther's protests, from which the term *Protestant* comes. Like him, they were tired of church corruption, particularly simony, which siphoned money out of

Germany and sent it to Rome. Further, they found the idea of personal salvation attractive. Thus, Lutheranism was enthusiastically taken up by large numbers of Germans, who then voluntarily left the Catholic Church.

The rapid spread of Lutheranism throughout Germany was aided by the printing press. As Durant notes, Luther and his followers used the new invention well:

Printing fell into his purpose as a seemingly providential innovation, which he used with inexhaustible skill; he was the first to make it an engine of propaganda. Battles were fought with books, pamphlets, and

letters intended for publication. Under the stimulus of Luther's revolt the number of books printed in Germany rose from 150 in 1518 to 990 in 1524. Four fifths of these favored the Reformation. [16]

A Divided Germany

Additionally, German politics favored Luther. Although technically known as the Holy Roman Empire, Renaissance Germany was not a unified domain but a loose collection of several hundred small states. The Holy Roman Emperor—the stoutly Catholic Charles V at this time—in theory controlled all these states. However, in reality, he lacked

German priest Martin Luther defies Rome by burning the papal decree that excommunicated him. Luther thus ignited the Protestant Reformation.

Luther Takes His Stand

In 1521, at a meeting in the German city of Worms, Emperor Charles V gave Martin Luther one last chance to renounce his position opposing the church. Luther explains his continued refusal in the following passage.

Your Imperial Majesty and Your Lordships demand a simple answer. Here it is, plain and unvarnished. Unless I am convicted [convinced] of error by the testimony of Scripture or (since I put no trust in the unsupported authority of Pope or councils, since it is plain that they have often erred and often contradicted themselves) by manifest reasoning, I stand convicted [convinced] by the Scriptures to which I have appealed, and my conscience is taken captive by God's word, I cannot and will not recant anything, for to act against our conscience is neither safe for us, nor open to us.

On this I take my stand. I can do no other. God help me.

Henry Bettenson, ed., *Document of the Christian Church.* 2nd ed. London: Oxford University Press, 1963.

any way of imposing his will on rebellious states. Thus, when northern and eastern states embraced Lutheranism, there was little Charles could do. Most western and southern states remained Catholic.

The states that became Lutheran did so for several reasons. First, their rulers often agreed with Luther's teachings. Second, they found rejection of the Catholic Church popular with their subjects. Finally, they found Lutheranism profitable. Breaking with the Catholic Church allowed a ruler to stop the flow of money out of his domain from simony. Further, these rulers often confiscated church property, such as monasteries, many of which owned large money-making estates.

The English Reformation

The Reformation soon spread outside Germany to other northern European domains in which discontent with the Catholic Church was widespread. Within a generation of Luther's Ninety-five Theses, Protestantism was the chief religion in Scandinavia, the Netherlands, Switzerland, and Scotland.

England also became a Protestant country, although for political rather than religious reasons. In the early 1530s English king Henry VIII petitioned Pope Clement VII for an annulment of his marriage to Catherine of Aragon. Henry wanted a male heir, and his only surviving child by Catherine was a daughter, Mary. After the annulment, he planned to marry a much younger woman, Anne

England's King Henry VIII introduces his new queen, Anne Boleyn, to court. The pope excommunicated Henry for the unlawful marriage so Henry declared himself head of the English church.

Boleyn. When the pope refused to annul the marriage, Henry had it annulled by the archbishop of Canterbury and then married Boleyn. The pope immediately excommunicated Henry, who, in 1534, declared himself the head of the church in England, which became known as the Anglican Church.

Henry did eventually have a son, but not with Anne, who gave him another daughter, Elizabeth. After having Boleyn convicted of adultery and executed, Henry married Jane Seymour, who produced a son, Edward. Upon Henry's death in 1547, Edward became king but died six years later, aged fifteen.

During Edward's short reign the kingdom remained Protestant, but when his Catholic sister, Mary, became queen in 1553, she restored the Catholic Church to England. Protestantism returned permanently as the state religion when Mary died in 1558 and her sister, Elizabeth, took the throne.

Differing Beliefs

No matter the nationality of Protestants, they had one thing in common: They rejected the Catholic Church's claim to be the one true Christian faith. However, they often disagreed on many other theological points. For instance, the church Luther founded and the Anglican Church retained many of the rituals and features of Catholicism. Thus, Lutherans and Anglicans still believed that the bread and wine of the communion service transformed into the flesh and blood of Jesus Christ. Another Protestant sect, the Calvinists, named for their chief architect, John Calvin, a French lawyer living in Geneva, dismissed such a transformation as superstition. To the Calvinists, the bread and wine were symbols and nothing more.

Further, unlike the Lutherans and the Anglicans, Calvinists believed in the elect: those pre-chosen by God to be saved. Like Catholics, many other Protestants believed that each individual had been given free will by God to choose a life of good or ill.

Death by Fire

Both Catholics and Protestants treated those accused of heresy in the same way: They executed them, frequently by burning alive. The following account, taken from John Foxe's 1563 Acts and Monuments, *describes the 1555 execution of the English Protestant clergyman Nicholas Ridley. Ridley's death occurred during the reign of Mary I, who, unlike her father, Henry VIII, remained a Catholic and actively suppressed Protestantism.*

By evil making of the fire, because the wood was overhigh built, the fire burned first beneath, being kept down by the wood so that it clean burned all his lower parts before it once touched the upper. After his legs were consumed by reason of his struggling with the pain (whereof he had no release) he showed his side towards us clean, shirt and all untouched with the flame; yet in all his torment he forgot not to call unto God, intermeddling this cry, "Let the fire come unto me." In which pangs he labored till one of the standersby with his pike pulled off the top wood, and where he spied the fire flame up, he wrested himself onto that side and was seen stir no more.

Hyder E. Rollins and Herchel Baker, eds., *The Renaissance of England: Non-Dramatic Prose and Verse of the Sixteenth Century.* Lexington, MA: Heath, 1954.

The Protestant Threat

The appeal of Protestantism was not confined to northern Europe. Protestants initially made inroads in France, although the kingdom remained primarily Catholic because a strong Catholic monarchy managed to contain and eventually expel most of the Protestants.

Additionally, French rulers had help from Rome in stamping out Protestantism. In 1542, to root out heresy in the church and to deal with Protestants and other dissenters in Catholic-dominated lands, Pope Paul III established the Inquisition. Made up of six cardinals, the Inquisition questioned suspects, sometimes

Both Catholic and Protestant authorities often condemned those they deemed heretics to be burned alive. Here, the condemned is led away.

Ignatius of Loyola kneels before the pope. Loyola founded the Society of Jesus, or Jesuits, a missionary order aimed at restoring and renewing the Catholic Church.

under torture, to determine their guilt or innocence. Those found guilty of heresy could be imprisoned or executed by hanging or burning alive.

The Counter-Reformation

Still, church officials realized that more was needed to protect the church than the Inquisition, for even in Italy, the heartland of Catholicism, there was a growing demand for church reform. Unlike northern Europe, as Durant points out, "the Italian argument was all for reform *with-*

in the church. And indeed, loyal churchmen had for centuries admitted the need for reform. The outbreak and progress of the Protestant Reformation gave new urgency to the need and the demand."[17]

The answer was a Catholic Counter-Reformation, and it came in the form of the Council of Trent, an assembly of church leaders convened by Pope Paul in 1545. Over the next eighteen years the council met three times and hammered out policies for directing and protecting the church. Above all else, the council made clear, according to John Hale, that "salvation was the result of faith in Christ and obedience to the Church's laws, with faith being confirmed by sincerely carried out good works of penance and charity."[18] Council members let stand the sale of indulgences. Beyond doctrine, the council recommended that priests be educated so that they could better fulfill their roles. Additional education was aimed at church members and was to instruct them in what they should believe and how they should act.

The Missionaries

The council also pushed for more missionary work. In Catholic lands these missionaries were to encourage Catholics whose faith was wavering and in Protestant territory to reconvert Protestants. The latter activity was dangerous, as Catholics were often subject to death if found preaching their faith in Protestant countries.

The most famous of the missionaries were the Jesuits, who were members of the Society of Jesus. Founded by Ignatius of Loyola in 1537, and thus predating the Council of Trent, the Jesuit order sent its missionaries not only all over Europe but also throughout the world. The Jesuits believed in converting by example. Thus, they lived humbly, with few possessions, and depended on donations for money. They saw themselves as spearheading the struggle for a renewed Catholic Church.

Religious Conflict

The last century of the Renaissance was marked by increasingly fierce religious persecution and war as Catholics and Protestants fought each other over their differing beliefs. Mary I of England, for instance, executed some three hundred Protestants, earning her the nickname "Bloody Mary," while her successor, Elizabeth I, put to death many Catholic missionaries, not the least of which were Jesuits.

Against this violent background Renaissance Europe continued to change in other ways. Among those changes the period saw important political upheavals that produced nations out of medieval kingdoms.

Chapter Three

The Growth of Nations

During the Renaissance a number of kingdoms transformed into nations, as monarchs consolidated power at the expense of their semi-independent nobility. By the end of the period such modern nations as Spain, France, and England had taken shape. As Crane Brinton observes, "We have here a picture [of Europe] that is not worlds apart from the present one."[19] These nations had central governments run by a corps of professional bureaucrats, along with established standing armies and diplomatic corps to promote and protect their interests.

The Rule of Monarchs

Because emerging nations of Europe were for the most part governed by a single ruler, they became known as national monarchies. Monarchies, such as France and England, had come out of the Middle Ages with the beginnings of central royal governments, and as the Renaissance progressed, the rulers of these countries strengthened their power base by putting more political authority in the hands of the crown.

This consolidation of royal power was often at the expense of the aristocracy in the various regions of each kingdom. Many of these local lords had enjoyed virtual independence during the Middle Ages, but now in the Renaissance they found themselves subject to the authority and commands of their monarch. As Charles G. Nauert writes:

> Royal authority grew because society needed strong government after an age in which aristocracy in all three countries had run wild. The nobles' control of government had set their class free to exploit their position as landlords, military commanders, and leading political figures in their home districts with a brutal disregard for the interests of

the state as a whole or its citizens. Relying on their own private armies, nobles seized other men's properties, conducted private warfare, and often acted the parts of bandits plundering the countryside. Since weak monarchy in every case was the most obvious cause of the nation's woes, a strengthened monarchy was the obvious solution. [20]

This new royal authority could be harsh. Renaissance rulers were a hard lot, acting out of ruthless self-interest. Almost all were willing to lie, cheat, steal, torture, and kill to keep and extend their individual power and authority. In 1513 the Italian Niccolò Machiavelli, who gave his name to the political philosophy of the age, wrote in his *Il principe* (*The Prince*):

> It must be understood that a prince [a ruler], and especially a new prince, cannot observe all those things which are considered good in men, being often obliged in order to maintain the state, to act against faith [to break promises], against charity, against humanity, and against religion. And, therefore, he must have a mind disposed to adapt itself according to the wind, and as the variations of fortune dictate, and do evil if necessary. [21]

France's King Louis XI epitomized the Machiavellian Renaissance ruler. He ruthlessly forged France into a unified nation.

Louis XI of France

The Machiavellian nature of Renaissance rulers is no better illustrated than in the character and actions of the French king Louis XI, who ruled from 1461 to 1483. Known as "the Universal Spider" because he was constantly spinning webs of intrigue, Louis began the transformation that turned a medieval kingdom of semi-independent states into a unified French nation.

Born in 1423, Louis started his scheming early. Impatient to become king, he began conspiring at seventeen against his father, Charles VII. His efforts left him in exile during Charles's last five years of life. During that exile Louis kept tabs on his father through a network of spies, a practice that led to rumors that he had had Charles poisoned. Whatever the truth of these rumors, Charles VII died in 1461, and Louis became king of France.

How to Rule

In The Prince *(1513) Niccolò Machiavelli discusses whether it is better for a ruler to be merciful and loved or cruel and feared.*

Every prince must desire to be considered merciful and not cruel. He must, however, take care not to misuse this mercifulness. A prince, therefore, must not mind incurring the charge of cruelty for the purpose of keeping his people united and faithful, for he will be more merciful than those who, from excess of tenderness, allow disorders to arise, from which spring bloodshed and rapine.

From this arises the question whether it is better to be loved more than feared, or feared more than loved. The reply is that one ought to be both feared and loved, but

as it is difficult for the two to go together, it is much safer to be feared than loved, if one of the two has to be wanting. It may be said of men in general that they are ungrateful and covetous of gain. And the prince who has relied entirely on their words [of loyalty], without making other preparations, is ruined. Men have less scruple in offending one who makes himself loved than one who makes himself feared.

Niccolò Machiavelli, *The Prince and the Discourses.* Trans. Luigi Ricci. Rev. E.R.P. Vincent. New York: Modern Library, 1950.

Niccolò Machiavelli's influential book The Prince *set the tone for the reigning political philosophy of his day.*

The Great Nobles

The new king was not much concerned with appearance or ceremony, openly ridiculing tradition and formality. He was stingy, refusing to spend money on himself. He wore cheap gray clothes and battered felt hats and ate the same plain food as the French peasants. His castles were dreary and dark, their furniture meager and shabby.

What concerned Louis was taming the aristocracy of France, and so upon taking the throne, his first act was to eliminate some of the ancient rights enjoyed by the most powerful nobles. Among other restrictions, he denied these local lords the right to mint their own money, make their own laws, and administer their own justice. He also outlawed the private wars that they fought among themselves. All of these practices were barriers to a united nation.

The great French nobles took poorly to Louis's commands, and many revolted. However, Louis eventually triumphed through a combination of war, diplomacy, and terror. The Spider King defeated some lords in battle and brought others around with promises of expansion of their lands. Still others he charged with treason and then either beheaded them or imprisoned them in iron cages, which were barely large enough to allow a prisoner to stand or sit. (The inventor of these cages spent fourteen years in one after offending Louis.)

Charles the Bold

The greatest challenge to the rule of Louis XI was posed by Charles the Bold, the Duke of Burgundy. Charles's militarily strong province arced from the North Sea to the Swiss border and contained portions of present-day northern and western France as well as Luxembourg, Belgium, and the Netherlands. Although a subject of the French king, Charles desired to break completely free of France and make Burgundy an independent kingdom with himself as monarch.

The struggle between Louis and Charles spanned a decade and a half. In the early years, victory went to Charles. In 1465 the duke trapped Louis in Paris and agreed to lift his siege of the city only in exchange for French land and money. Three years later Charles captured Louis, and the French monarch achieved his freedom only in exchange for more land and money. However, in 1470 the balance began to swing in favor of the French king when Louis destroyed an alliance that Charles had made with King Edward IV of England to help him in the ongoing conflict. Louis simply bribed the English monarch to abandon Charles.

Three years later Louis convinced Switzerland that it was in danger from Charles's ambitions for his own kingdom and then agreed to pay for a Swiss war against Burgundy. In 1477, after fighting and losing two previous battles with the Swiss, Charles was killed while engaged in a third.

Since the duke left no male heir, his lands were broken up. The duke's daughter inherited Belgium and the Netherlands, and Louis successfully claimed much of the rest of Burgundy, including the lands that Charles had extorted from him a decade earlier.

The Tudors of England

Other European monarchs followed in the footsteps of Louis XI. Beginning with Henry VII in 1485, the English royal family, the Tudors, started curbing their own nobility. Particularly troublesome aristocrats were executed. The Tudors then gave the titles of the dead to newly cre-

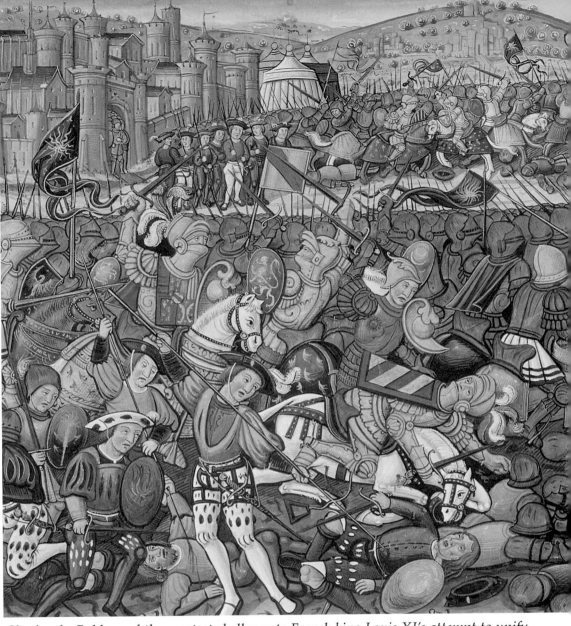

Charles the Bold posed the greatest challenge to French king Louis XI's attempt to unify France, but Charles's death in battle gave Louis free rein.

ated nobles, who tended to be grateful to the royal family for their rank and thus loyal to the English monarchy.

Somewhat milder but no less effective in dealing with the English aristocracy were the proceedings of the Star Chamber, a court named for the stars painted on its chamber's ceiling. The Star Chamber targeted those nobles reluctant to submit to the English crown. This court lacked the authority to sentence the convicted to death, but it could fine them heavily as well as imprison, brand, and even mutilate them.

Forging the Monarchy of Spain

As France and England moved toward nationhood, a national monarchy was also rising in Spain. In some ways the Spanish rulers had an advantage over their fellow monarchs, for they were working with a country that had only just come into existence. Spain had not been united until 1479, when Aragon and Castile, two of the three kingdoms occupying the Spanish peninsula, finally became one under the joint rule of King Ferdinand of Aragon and Queen Isabella of Castile (the third kingdom, Portugal, remained independent). Together, the king and queen built a new government that favored the monarchy.

One of Ferdinand and Isabella's first acts was the creation of the Corps of Gentlemen of the King's House and Guard, which was responsible for running the kingdom. The Corps, however, only had as much authority as the king and queen allowed it. Ferdinand and Isabella staffed

King Ferdinand (on throne, right) and Queen Isabella cunningly organized the Spanish government to take power from the nobility and give it to the monarchy.

the Corps with aristocrats, who thus spent their time working for the king and queen's interest rather than their own. As an added benefit, the Spanish monarchs could also keep a close eye on these nobles.

The two monarchs undermined the power of the aristocracy in other ways as well. Castile had three orders, or fraternities, of nobles, any or all of which could have become the core of an aristocratic rebellion. Isabella persuaded each order to elect Ferdinand as its head. In this way the king and queen gained control of these potential sources of rebellion and turned them into supporters of the royal government.

The two monarchs also formed alliances with various Spanish towns against local aristocrats. Town militia, rather than aristocratic warriors, became the source of troops for the kingdom's defense. This alliance between town and crown was not perfect since the monarchs began meddling in each town's government by sending royal inspectors and administrators. However, in the long run the towns prospered as the new central government brought stability to Spain.

Ferdinand and Isabella did their work well, leaving to their successors the foundation for a strong central Spanish government. According to Ernst Breisach, "under the leadership of Isabella and Ferdinand, Spain became the monarchy in which the most consistent and rapid centralization of power in royal hands took place. Royal power began to prevail over the so-called traditional rights of the nobles."[22]

Leonardo Bruni and the Active Life

The rulers of other western European states also sought to imitate the success of the monarchs of France, England, and Spain. Thus, national monarchies arose in Spain's neighbor Portugal and farther north in the Scandinavian countries of Denmark, Norway, and Sweden. Additionally, though not monarchies, many of the city-states of Italy saw the concentration of power into the hands of a single ruler, much in the manner of the national monarchies.

In all of this political evolution, humanism played a role. Although Petrarch and most other early humanists were strictly scholars and had little to do with public affairs, some later humanists took important positions as government officials. For instance, the humanist Sir Thomas More became the chief administrator for the English monarchy.

This political humanism was first promoted in the early fifteenth century by the Italian Leonardo Bruni, who called it "the active life." Bruni was a noted scholar of his day. His Latin translations of Aristotle, Plato, and other Greek authors made the works of these writers readily available to those who did not read Greek.

Bruni, however, was not content to study. He felt that his learning and knowledge must be applied to the world he saw around him, and he thus urged his fellow humanists to lead an active public life. Bruni took as his model the Roman statesman Cicero. According to the Italian humanist, Cicero had achieved an ideal balance between scholarly and political activities and "was the only man to have fulfilled both of these great and difficult accomplishments."[23]

Humanism and the State

Humanists were well suited to government work. Many were trained as lawyers, and all were schooled in rhetoric and languages. Nauert notes that "the arts of eloquent and persuasive speech and writing were useful to any government, and so the most distinguished and successful humanists of the fifteenth and sixteenth centuries were hired to employ these arts."[24]

Even humanists who did not actually hold a government post made political contributions to their homelands by supplying models to justify the rule of strong Renaissance monarchs. They found these models in descriptions of classical Greek monarchies and in writings on the Roman Empire. Humanists also wrote histories, poems, and plays in praise of ruling families.

A number of Renaissance rulers were themselves humanists. The sixteenth century saw Francis I, who loved letters and the arts, open the humanist College of France. During the same century England's Henry VIII and his daughter Elizabeth I were enthusiastic sponsors of scholarship and the arts as well as powerful rulers intent upon consolidating political authority.

The Donation of Constantine

Occasionally humanistic scholarship itself became a tool of statecraft, as in the case of the Donation of Constantine. The donation was supposedly a grant from the fourth-century Roman emperor Constantine giving the pope authority over much of Italy. In 1440, citing the Donation of Constantine, Pope Eugenius IV went to war with Alfonso V, king of Aragon. Both claimed to be the rightful ruler of Naples; Eugenius based his claim on the donation, and Alfonso's claim was supported by the fact that he had been adopted by the previous ruler of Naples.

Lorenzo Valla, whose patron was Alfonso, was suspicious of the authenticity of the Donation of Constantine. By comparing the document with classical works from Constantine's period, Valla was able to show that both the Latin used and the historical references made were from a time centuries after Constantine's death. His conclusions were so convincing that the Donation of Constantine was utterly discredited, thus ending the pope's claimed authority over Naples or any other Italian city-state. By showing that the Donation of Constantine was a forgery, Valla had extended the power of humanism beyond the study walls.

The Military

As with Eugenius and Alfonso, the ambitions of Renaissance rulers often brought them into conflict. Power struggles between states were a hallmark of the age. These struggles frequently erupted into war and led to the creation of the modern army, which was always on duty and always prepared to fight and whose ranks were filled with full-time, paid, professional soldiers. Such standing armies

The Pope and Naples

The complexity of Italian politics is revealed in the following 1489 letter, in which Lorenzo de' Medici advised Pope Innocent VIII on how best to unseat Naples' King Ferrante. According to Innocent, Ferrante owed the papacy money.

His Holiness should decide on following one of three paths: enforce his will by war against the King, or come to some agreement, or, if an honorable agreement is not possible at the present, to temporize [compromise] in a dignified way, and wait for a better occasion. The first is not possible to achieve without putting a new ruler over the Kingdom of Naples. For this, according to my views, either Venice or Milan must be a party to the enterprise, supposing always that Venice adheres to the plan and would prevent Milan from helping the King. From what I understand there is no reason that His Holiness should at the present time have this plan or hope, for either Spain or France must be made to intervene to achieve this purpose. Spain does not appear to me strong enough, particularly, as regards money. What reliance is to be placed on France, seeing the French nature [a weak king]?

Lorenzo de' Medici, *Lorenzo de' Medici: Selected Poems and Prose.* Ed. and trans. Jon Thiem. University Park: Pennsylvania State University Press, 1991.

had not existed in western Europe since the days of the Roman Empire. The first of these professional armies was established in France in 1439, and within a century a few seafaring countries, such as Spain, had also built navies.

The Renaissance army, like its modern counterpart, was divided into ranks of officers and common soldiers. Officers were normally members of the aristocracy, while soldiers belonged to the peasant class. Just as in today's armies, officers drilled their soldiers, teaching them how to parade, dress ranks, and keep discipline, all part of the process of making the army a reliable fighting force.

During this period no army supplied its members with uniforms. Individual units, however, often dressed alike. Since fighting was often hand to hand, soldiers were armed with swords and long pikes. Some units were issued primitive guns, although these were difficult to use because early models were big, clumsy weapons that were not very accurate.

Diplomats

The same Renaissance power struggles that gave birth to the modern army also created the modern diplomat. Breisach writes that the "continuous maneuvering for power became an important stimulus for the development of diplomacy. Governments simply needed channels of communication, facilities for information gathering, and opportunities to make their influence felt abroad."[25]

The chief means to these diplomatic ends was for a government to have ambassadors living in other countries. These resident Renaissance ambassadors acted as their government's agent or representative, looking after their country's interests abroad. They also sent home regular reports, detailing political and social trends in the host countries as well as describing the character and personalities of local officials and rulers. The importance of these reports is reflected in how often they were intercepted and stolen by agents of other governments. Such theft eventually required that ambassadorial reports be written in code.

As Renaissance diplomacy evolved, European states worked out rules governing the relations among themselves. Out of these rules grew modern international law. For instance, by the end of the Renaissance ambassadors and their staffs had achieved some of the privileges common to resident diplomats today. Each was immune to the laws and taxes of the host country, and the ambassador's living quarters were considered to be a part of his native land.

Invading Italy

Diplomacy was not merely used to stop or to prevent conflicts in Renaissance Europe, it also was considered necessary in order to fight a war. A state that wanted to launch a war had first to protect its

own borders. If it did not, neighboring domains might use such a war as a golden opportunity to invade while the warring country's army was occupied elsewhere.

Thus, in 1494, when the French king Charles VIII, son of Louis XI, invaded Italy, he first safeguarded his kingdom

France's King Charles VIII marches triumphantly into Florence, Italy. The ease of Charles's victory alarmed his ally Ferdinand of Spain, who then sided against him.

through separate treaties with England and Spain. King Henry VII of England received a yearly sum of fifty thousand francs, and King Ferdinand of Spain was given title to land between France and his realm. Both monarchs pledged to leave France in peace during Charles's Italian campaign.

Such agreements, however, could be short-lived, as that between Charles and

Ferdinand proved to be. The Spanish king became alarmed at the speed and ease of the French army's passage through Italy. He felt that such an easy victory would strengthen France and fuel Charles's ambition. Thus, the Spanish monarch banded together with Milan and Venice to drive the French back out of Italy.

Bureaucrats

Later French adventures in Italy involved France allying itself with Venice against Milan and joining with Spain to capture Naples. In the latter case the French and Spanish fell to fighting each other over the division of the spoils.

Such constant warfare and shifting alliances gave much work to Renaissance diplomats, for in addition to resident ambassadors, the governments of Renaissance Europe required diplomats to attend peace talks and draw up treaties. Eventually each state came to need a specialized governmental department with full-time staffs, whose job it was to monitor foreign affairs.

Likewise, other aspects of government came increasingly under the management of a professional bureaucracy. For instance, royal revenues of each national monarchy were under the control of a state treasury. Needing a record-keeping agency, England formed a department called the chancery, meaning secretary. Modeled on an office that served the pope, this department kept the records of all royal laws, rulings, and transactions. France and Spain maintained similar offices.

In order to ensure the loyalty of these bureaucrats, monarchs paid them a salary. This practice differed from that of the Middle Ages, during which royal advisers and aides were given farming estates or other money-producing enterprises, known as fiefs, in payment for their services. A salary made royal administrators completely dependent for their livelihood on the goodwill of the monarch, whereas fiefholders who fell out of favor could live off the profits from their fiefs. In addition, a salary, unlike a fief, was not hereditary, allowing the king to remove bureaucrats who proved incompetent or troublesome.

To finance these various government departments, not to mention the many wars and diplomatic missions of the period, took money. And the money was there because western Europe of the Renaissance was prosperous, its wealth coming mainly from trade and banking.

Chapter Four

A World of Business

The Renaissance was an age of flourishing commerce and prosperity, and Renaissance society unapologetically reveled in its wealth. Not everyone, of course, shared in the riches; there was still much poverty and the hardship that poverty brings. However, for the aristocracy and the growing middle class, wealth flowed from all sorts of businesses, with fortunes made particularly in trading and banking. Trade and the merchants who controlled it exerted great influence over the policies and fates of European states. In like manner, banks and bankers were equally powerful and influential.

Humanism and Wealth

Much of the wealth of Renaissance Europe was in the hands of the middle or business class. In general, wealthy Renaissance Europeans enjoyed their prosperity, openly boasting of the luxuries they could afford to buy. This outspoken materialism was in marked contrast to traditional Christian teachings, which still held that virtue came from self-denial and poverty. Many Renaissance Europeans, however, rejected the idea that virtue was tied to poverty. They saw nothing wrong with being rich and with showy displays of wealth in the form of expensive clothing, furnishings, and art.

This Renaissance materialism was strongly supported by a number of humanists. The Italian humanist Gian Francesco Poggio Bracciolini wrote in his 1428 *De avaritia* (*Of Avarice*) that wanting money and property served a useful social role because it made people work. Other humanists believed that the desire for money was a normal part of human nature and that trade and money were essential in building and maintaining civilization. Ernst Breisach observes:

> Some humanists gave powerful support to contemporary economic activities and of the accumulation

Two Italian Renaissance cloth merchants measure a bolt of cloth. A business boom brought great wealth to a burgeoning middle class that embraced materialism.

of wealth. A good example is the humanist answer to the traditional call of purists for poverty as the ideal Christian condition. Far from condemning the possession of property many humanists emphasized the increased opportunities for being virtuous which became available to those of means. [The fifteenth-century humanist] Leon Battista Alberti succinctly stated that man needs a home, property, and a job to be fully a man.[26]

Critics of Materialism

Not all humanists approved of the widespread materialism of the period. Erasmus and others among the northern Christian humanists thought Europe was caught in the grip of pure and simple greed. In 1508 the Dutch scholar wrote that "nowadays the rage for possession has got to such a pitch that there is nothing out of which profit cannot be squeezed."[27] Martin Luther went further, saying that large profits were a form of theft, with the merchant stealing from the customer. From Switzerland the Protestant reformer John Calvin warned that to be overly concerned with money was to place one's soul in danger.

However, such opposition to the period's materialism had little effect. Indeed, even the critics were attracted to the prosperous life. Erasmus had a portrait painted that showed him wearing the clothes of a successful merchant, and Calvin and his followers eventually came to see wealth as a sign of an individual being favored by God. All over Europe there were many opportunities to make money and plenty of people ready to seize those opportunities.

The Business of Trade

Much of this wealth and prosperity was based on trade. Among the items most eagerly traded in the Renaissance were the raw materials needed to make clothing, ships, glassware, wine, beer, soap, and gunpowder. Thus, wool from England became finished cloth in Belgium and the Netherlands. Raw glass from the Middle East was turned into decorative glassware in Venice and other Italian cities. Timber from the Baltic and the Middle East provided the lumber to build the ships of trade and exploration. The largest profits generally came from marketing such luxury items as furs and silks.

Successful merchants grew enormously rich as their businesses expanded, trading first with other European regions and then with the Middle East, Asia, and finally the Americas. According to Will Durant, in pursuit of profit, these merchants became great travelers: "They moved with their goods, often they traveled great distances to buy cheaply where the products they wanted abounded, and returned to sell dear where their goods were rare. . . . These merchants were adventurers, explorers, knights of the caravan, armed with daggers and bribes, ready for highwaymen, pirates, and a thousand tribulations." [28]

The Hanseatic League

Successful merchants came to dominate both the growing middle class and the local governments. Some merchants, banding together in associations, even became regional powers, as did those along the coast of the Baltic Sea. In the thirteenth century, to control a profitable trade and protect it from pirates and bandits, the cities of northern

Glassblowers ply their trade in Renaissance Italy. Venetian artisans became famous for their decorative glassware.

Germany formed a trading alliance called the Hanseatic League, which took its name from the German *Hanse,* meaning "association" or "company." At its height the league numbered close to a hundred towns, led by Lübeck, Hamburg, and Daniz.

The merchants of the Hanseatic League reaped most of their profits from food. Wheat from the rich farmlands of northeastern Europe was shipped to England and the rest of western Europe. The other major trade item was salted herring, which was prized because it did not spoil easily, could be shipped long distances, and was cheap. Historian Emil Lucki writes that "the catch was rich, the packing cheap because of the accessibility to abundant supplies of timber for barrels, the market close by, and the demand extensive. Profits were substantial."[29] In addition to wheat and salted herring, the Hanseatic League sent wax, timber, tar, pitch, furs, and copper west. To the east it brought wool, wine, salt, and silver.

The Power of the Hanse

Although it had no formal government, the members of the Hanseatic League assembled when necessary to decide policy; portion out money for joint ventures, particularly military campaigns; make and ratify treaties; and dispatch diplomats. The Hanse also had final say over laws and regulations that were to be adopted by each town that belonged to the league.

The league even had its own legal code and flag. More importantly, it had warships and soldiers with which it fought to keep its tight grip on its trade goods and routes. In 1370, for instance, the league defeated Denmark after the Danish king Valdemar IV had harassed Hanse shipping and then attacked a league town. The Treaty of Stralsund that ended the fighting freed the Hanse from

This manuscript illumination shows the bustling Hanse port of Hamburg, Germany, a member of the Hanseatic League.

In Praise of Wealth

The Italian humanist Leonardo Bruni argues in support of Renaissance materialism in his notes to his 1445 translation of Aristotle's Economics.

Aristotle says that the head of the household must therefore be of an acquisitive nature, that is, the kind of man who will be quick and skillful at making a profit. This, then, is a talent that the head of the household should possess above all others, that is making a profit from the fruits of his estates and other business.

The remaining two talents that the head of the household must possess are how to make his wealth an adornment, and to enjoy it. For these two purposes, wealth is useful. Not that it is seemly to make ourselves its slaves, but to turn it to our service. Wealth will lend adornment and honor if we make our outlays wisely and gracefully. These will include building a house in keeping with our wealth, having a good staff of servants, sufficient furniture, a decent array of horses and clothing. They will also include generosity to friends and patronage of public events.

Leonardo Bruni, *The Humanism of Leonardo Bruni: Selected Texts.* Trans. Gordon Griffiths, James Hankins, and David Thompson. Binghamton, NY: Renaissance Society of America, 1987.

paying Denmark's custom duties, gave it virtual control over several Danish cities for five years, and allowed it a hand in selecting the next king of Denmark.

Later, in 1406, English fishermen tried to invade the fishing grounds of the Baltic. The Hanse took swift and direct action, sending a fleet that captured almost a hundred English fishermen. The German captains then had the fishermen bound hand and foot and tossed overboard to drown.

The Hanse in Decline

By the mid–fifteenth century Hanseatic power in the Baltic was dwindling. This decline was caused partly by a shift in fishing grounds. The herring, that up to that time had lived and bred in the Baltic, moved for some unknown reason into the North Sea, outside of Hanse control.

The major cause of the league's decline, however, was internal. Rivalries among various league towns and jealousies among the Hanse's most powerful merchants sapped Hanseatic power. Loyalty to the league ran a distant second to each member's self-interest.

The divided league was unable to cope with the rise of strong rivals, such as the kingdoms of Lithuania and Poland, as well as a union of Denmark, Sweden, and Norway. The Hanse, handicapped by its bickering members, could not respond swiftly enough to counter the moves of its better-organized competitors. Finally, in the middle of the sixteenth century the Hanseatic League was given a death blow when the Dutch grabbed away the last of the east-west Baltic trade from the Hanse.

Venice: City of Merchants

South, in the Mediterranean, another trade empire flourished: the city-state of Venice. Indeed, few merchants were as politically powerful as those in this northern Italian city-state. Unlike the Hanse, much of Venice's profits came from the import of luxury goods. In the Middle East the Venetians traded western wool, lead, and tin for dyes, silk, spices, sugar, and cotton. Some of the Middle Eastern trade goods were originally from Asia, imported from as far away as China along centuries-old land routes.

Commerce transformed and supported Venice's political organization. The city-state had once been ruled by a doge, or duke, elected by Venetian citizens. But during the Renaissance actual political control was in the hands of a select group of the oldest merchant families, who, as members of the Great Council, appointed the officials who formed the government. The Great Council, instead of the Venetian citizens, now elected the doge, who became a figurehead overseeing official ceremonies and entertaining important foreign visitors.

Venice was by no means the only Italian city-state engaged in Mediterranean trade. Genoa, situated on Italy's west coast, amassed a trading empire that almost matched that of Venice. The rival-ry of Venice and Genoa for the lucrative eastern trade led first to competition for goods and markets, then to friction, and finally to war. In 1380 the Venetians emerged triumphant when they captured the Genoese fleet, a blow from which Genoa never recovered. By the beginning of the fifteenth century, as Robert Ergang notes, Venice "was the richest city in Europe with an income larger than that of [whole] kingdoms. It also had a fleet of warships larger than any other Christian power."[30]

As the Renaissance progressed, however, Venice found itself in trouble. In the late fifteenth century the city-state began to lose control of its Asian and Middle Eastern trade routes, which were blocked by the Ottoman Empire that now ruled the entire eastern Mediterranean. Whenever possible, the Ottoman Turks hindered Venetian trading, and Venice found itself fighting a series of costly wars with the Turks.

To India and the New World

A second and even more damaging threat to Venice was the rise of trade rivals in western Europe. Both Portugal and Spain were anxious to grab a share of the lucrative eastern trade. Blocked by both Venice and the Ottoman Empire from the eastern Mediterranean, these countries sought other ways of reaching Asia.

In 1421 Portugal's Prince Henry, known as the Navigator, began sending ships south in search of a way around Africa to Asia. Despite his title of Navigator, Henry himself did not go exploring but rather

Portuguese explorer Vasco da Gama's successful voyage to India opened trade and brought great wealth to Portugal.

arranged financing for voyages of exploration. He also established a school for navigation and mapmaking at Sagres on Cape St. Vincent, the rocky southernmost tip of Portugal.

Even after Henry's death Portuguese ships continued their explorations, traveling ever farther south along the African coast and making detailed maps as they went. Finally, in 1488, Bartholomeu Diaz de Novaes rounded the Cape of Good Hope. Ten years later, following Diaz de Novaes's lead, a Portuguese expedition commanded by Vasco da Gama reached India.

In the late fifteenth century Portugal's neighbor Spain also wanted to find a sea route to Asia, but barred by the Portuguese from exploring south, Spain looked west. In 1492 the Italian Christopher Columbus, sailing for King Ferdinand and Queen Isabella, made landfall on islands in the Americas.

Spices and Slaves

Both Portugal and Spain became wealthy and powerful by exploiting the accomplishments of their explorers. Portugal followed Da Gama's voyage with trading missions and was soon importing spices and other luxury goods from India. In 1503 Portuguese traders reached Indonesia, the source of many spices, such as cloves, nutmeg, and pepper, and they began sending back huge shipments of these valuable seasonings.

But even before Diaz de Novaes rounded the Cape of Good Hope, Portuguese sailors had found a moneymaking business—slavery. In 1441 the first

African slaves arrived in Europe, beginning the centuries-long African slave trade, which resulted in the enslavement of millions of people.

Gold and Silver

The Spanish in the New World had found another type of treasure—gold and silver. Much of this gold and silver was in the possession of two great native American civilizations, the Aztec of Mexico and the Inca of Peru, and this possession led to the conquest of the former in 1521 by Hernán Cortés and of the latter in 1533 by Francisco Pizarro.

Both cultures had created excellent golden and silver artwork and jewelry. However, much of it, weighing in the tons, was melted down by the conquerors and shipped back to Spain. When the artifacts ran out, the Spanish used Indian and African slaves to mine for both gold and silver; the silver mines of Peru became major sources of wealth for Spain for the duration of the Renaissance.

Trade and Sea Dogs

Other Atlantic-facing countries—France, England, and the Netherlands—were also interested in opening overseas trade routes and by the early fifteenth century were sending ships to buy and sell Asian goods at Portuguese outposts in Africa. Trade with the Spanish in the New World was more difficult because it was illegal for Spanish settlers to buy from or sell to foreign ships. All such trade was supposed to be done in Spain so that the Spanish government could exercise tight control, thus protecting the crown's share of the profits.

Spanish explorer Francisco Pizarro conquers the Peruvian Inca in this painting. Spain's attempt to reach India by sailing west garnered it the riches of the Americas instead.

Some illegal trade with Spanish settlements was possible but not enough to satisfy English sailors, who took to attacking and looting Spanish ships and colonies. These English raiders, known as "sea dogs," were commanded by such captains as Sir John Hawkins and Sir Francis Drake, who made their backers wealthy with plundered Spanish gold and silver. Among the sponsors of the sea dogs was the English queen Elizabeth I.

The Spanish Armada

Tensions ran high between England and Spain over the raids of Drake and others.

To the English the sea dogs were heroes, but to the Spanish they were pirates. Eventually the raids, along with other issues, particularly religious ones since England was Protestant and Spain Catholic, led to war.

The Spanish king, Philip II, decided to invade England, so he assembled a fleet of some 130 warships. Known as the Invincible or Spanish Armada, Philip's fleet fought a series of battles with the smaller English navy in the English Channel during the first week of August 1588. These engagements went poorly for the Spanish, whose ships were outmaneuvered by the

Affliction at Sea

Lengthy Renaissance sea voyages were dangerous affairs, as this account by an anonymous member of the Vasco da Gama expedition reveals. The expedition, becalmed for much of three months before finally reaching land, suffered from scurvy, caused by a lack of vitamin C.

Our people suffered from their gums, which drew over their teeth, so they could not eat. Their legs also swelled, and other parts of the body, and these swellings spread until the sufferer died, without exhibiting symptoms of any other disease. Thirty of our men died in this manner, and those able to navigate were only seven or eight, and even these were not as well as they ought to have been. I assure you that if this state of affairs had continued for another fortnight [two weeks] there would have been no men at all to navigate the ships.

Ronald Watkins, *Unknown Seas: How Vasco da Gama Opened the East.* London: Murray, 2003.

English. Finally, defeated and blocked from returning south to Spain, the badly mauled Armada sailed north around Britain, where it ran headlong into a series of storms that shipwrecked or sank many of the survivors. Only about half the Armada returned to Spain; the English did not lose a single ship. Although the defeat of the Armada was a blow to Spain, it was far from a mortal one as the country still had its colonial empire and all the wealth contained therein.

Banking

All European trade was intimately linked to the other great moneymaking enterprise of the Renaissance: banking. The banks of the period grew out of coin exchanges, which were needed because the great trading centers, such as Venice and the Hanseatic League, brought in not only goods from other parts of Europe but also foreign currency. More than two hundred currencies floated through Europe during the Renaissance, and few merchants could keep track of relative rates of exchange, preferring to consult experts at the coin exchanges.

Coin exchanging became true banking with the acceptance and safeguarding of deposits and the issuance of loans for profit. These Renaissance banks also offered another important service: They arranged for funds to be transferred from different regions. The bankers of the time did many of these transfers on paper, thus reducing the need to ship actual money from place to place. Such shipments always ran the risk of being lost through either accident or banditry.

The Bankers of Florence

During the early Renaissance the most important bankers, called the Lombard bankers, were located in northern Italy. The center of this Lombard banking industry was Florence with its eighty great financial houses, the most powerful being owned by the Medici. Most of these Florentine firms were located on a single street called Evil Street, not because of the banks' reputations but because the street had once been the haunt of murderers and thieves. The banks of Florence soon opened branches in other parts of Italy and Europe. The Medici firm alone established sixteen branches during the fifteenth century.

Florence at its height was richer than the largest kingdoms of Renaissance Europe. Its gold florin became an international coin good anywhere in Europe or the Middle East. The florin financed not only Renaissance businesses but also the operations of the Catholic Church and the wars of various European countries. Durant observes:

> The eighty banking houses of Florence—chiefly the Bardi, Peruzzi, Strozzi, Pitti, and Medici—invested the savings of their depositors. They cashed checks (*polizze*), issued letters of credit (*lettere di pagamenti*), exchanged merchandise as well as credit, and supplied governments with funds for peace and war. . . . Florence became the financial capital of Europe from the thirteenth through the fifteenth century; it was there that the rates of exchange were fixed for the currencies of Europe.[31]

The so-called Invincible Armada of Spain proved to be anything but, as its invasion of England was roundly repelled and its ships destroyed.

In addition to financing the great merchants of the period, most of the Florentine banking houses also engaged in some trade. The Medici, for instance, traded in wool and silk.

Medici Rule

By the fourteenth century the bankers of Florence had gained political control of their city-state, and from 1434 to well into the eighteenth century, rule of Florence belonged to the Medici. For the first century of Medici management the family rarely held an actual office. Rather, they preferred to work behind the scenes, exerting their influence through a complex web of favors and bribes, the latter normally given in the form of generous loans from their bank. In 1429 Giovanni di Bicii de' Medici told his family to "not appear to give advice, but put your views forward discreetly in conversation. Avoid litigation and political controversy, and always keep out of the public eye."[32]

The influence of these behind-the-scenes rulers extended far beyond the walls of Florence. Medici money paid for the lavish

A fifteenth-century woodcut portrays a Florentine banking house. Florence was the banking capital of Europe during the Renaissance.

courts of many European monarchs and financed those same monarchs' wars and trading ventures. Consequently, in both Florence and beyond, when a Medici made a suggestion, it often was heard as a command. In 1459 Pope Pius II observed of Cosimo de' Medici, "Political questions are settled at his house. The man he chooses holds office. He it is who decides the peace and war and controls the laws. He is King in everything but name."[33]

In the early sixteenth century the Medici gave up their pretense of being just ordinary citizens of Florence, and the senior member of the family became first the duke of Florence and then of Tuscany, the larger region surrounding the city. Throughout the Renaissance the Medici remained powerful, and this power was used to make four of them pope and two of them queen of France, positions that gave the family even greater influence throughout western Europe.

One of the universal characteristics of the Medici family was enthusiasm for art, philosophy, and literature. Family members were among the greatest patrons of the Renaissance. However, they were far from being alone, for most Renaissance rulers sought to attract the most accomplished artists and thinkers of the day to their courts. The French king Francis I, for example, was the patron of the Italian master Leonardo da Vinci. Indeed, Renaissance courts and royal money, some of it coming from Asian and New World revenues, were the major supports of the arts in western Europe.

Chapter Five

Artists and Musicians

The Renaissance was an era of enthusiastic experimentation in art and music. In the visual arts, such experimentation led to the discovery of perspective and the first use of oil paints. Music saw the introduction of more complex melodies with the use of counterpoint and the invention of a number of new instruments. Both Renaissance artists and musicians left a rich legacy of work, with painting and sculpture perhaps representing the glory of the Renaissance more than any other accomplishment.

The Changing Arts

If any one aspect of Renaissance culture differed markedly from the Middle Ages, it was art. During the Middle Ages the arts had reflected that period's deep interest in religion. Paintings, for instance, were either portraits of Jesus, Mary, and the saints or illustrations of scenes from the Bible.

However, in the Renaissance art became less religious in nature. Much of it dealt with more worldly subjects, portraits of living people, landscapes, and scenes of everyday life. Religious subjects did not disappear. Indeed, some of the greatest religious art dates from the Renaissance, such as Leonardo da Vinci's 1498 painting *The Last Supper* and Michelangelo's 1504 sculpture *David*.

Yet there was a more secular tone to Renaissance art than to medieval art. This artistic shift came in part because the patrons of artists were often business and civil leaders rather than, as in the Middle Ages, the church. These patrons were generally interested in having themselves or their families immortalized in paint or stone.

Additionally, the concerns of Renaissance art were influenced by humanism, with its interest in antiquity and Greek and Roman myths. Many Renaissance paintings and sculptures were of classical subjects, such as Sandro Botticelli's *The Birth of Venus* (ca. 1480).

The Premier Arts

A second difference between Renaissance and medieval art was the supreme importance of architecture during the Middle Ages. To the medieval world, architecture was the most majestic of arts because architects were responsible for the design and building of the great cathedrals and churches of the period. At this time both painting and sculpture were used almost exclusively to decorate these church buildings.

In the Renaissance, however, although architecture remained important, painting and sculpture were the chief arts. Again, this change in emphasis had a great deal to do with the rise of the pri-vate patron, few of whom, like the Catholic Church, could afford to finance a building but any one of whom could pay for a painting or a statue.

Painters and sculptors benefited socially from the attention patrons paid their arts. During the Middle Ages and into the early Renaissance, artists were considered tradespeople, not unlike carpenters and masons. This changed as the Renaissance progressed. As Ernst Breisach writes:

Lay patrons began to use art for enhancing their social prestige and status and for sheer enjoyment. As they used works of art for their conspicuous possession, artists benefited from it by enhancement of their own status. Artistic gifts found a

Perhaps no other work of art says "the Renaissance" like Da Vinci's Last Supper. *Despite the secular nature of Renaissance art, great artists often chose religious subjects to depict.*

new appreciation and artists gradually occupied a position apart and higher than other craftsmen. Artistic activity came to be regarded as one worthy of serious consideration.[34]

A Realistic Art

A third difference between medieval and Renaissance art was the latter's emphasis on realism. Renaissance artists tried to represent the human figure as realistically and naturally as possible. To achieve this realism, both painters and sculptors studied anatomy and the world around them. They worked hard to portray their painted or sculpted subjects in authentic detail. As the Italian Leon Battista Alberti instructs in his 1435 *Della pittura* (*On Painting*):

It will help, when painting living creatures, first to sketch in the bones, for as they bend very little indeed, they always occupy a certain determined position. Then add the sinews and muscles, and finally clothe the bones and muscles with flesh and skin. As Nature clearly and openly reveals all these proportions, so the zealous painter will find great profit from investigating them in Nature.[35]

The Importance of Painting

In the course of his very technical book On Painting, *written in 1435, Leon Battista Alberti stops to explain why painting is so important.*

As the effort of learning may perhaps seem to the young too laborious, I think I should explain here how painting is worthy of all our intention and study. Painting possesses a truly divine power in that not only does it make the absent present (as they say of friendship), but it also represents the dead to the living many centuries later, so that they are recognized by spectators with pleasure and deep admiration for the artist. Plutarch tells us that Cassandrus, one of Alexander the Great's commanders, trembled all over at the sight of a portrait of the deceased Alexander. How much painting contributes to the honest pleasures of the mind, and to the beauty of things, may be seen in various ways but especially in the fact that you will find nothing so precious which association with painting does not render far more valuable and highly praised. Ivory, gems, and all other similar precious things are made more valuable by the hand of the painter.

Leon Battista Alberti, *On Painting*. Trans. Cecil Grayson. London: Penguin, 1972.

Critics hailed Donatello's bronze sculpture of the biblical king David as a masterpiece of realism.

Because of its close association with the observation of the natural world, this Renaissance realism came to be known as naturalism.

One of the pioneers of Renaissance naturalism was the painter Giotto di Bondone. Born in 1267, Giotto was a native of Florence and a tireless experimenter in technique. His innovations included adding emotions, such as grief, joy, and boredom, to the faces of the people in his paintings. He also dressed his subjects in the everyday clothing he saw about him.

Among sculptors, Donato de Betto di Bardi, who was born in 1386 and is better known by his nickname Donatello, was instrumental in promoting naturalism.

Living much of his life in Florence under the patronage of Cosimo de' Medici, Donatello was one of the first Renaissance artists to work in bronze rather than stone. But no matter what the material used, he labored to give his sculptures realistic details in order to capture the human personality of his subjects. The realism of Donatello's work led the sixteenth-century art historian Giorgio Vasari to exclaim in his 1550 *Vite de' più eccellenti architetti, pittori, et scultori italiani* (*Lives of the Most Excellent Italian Architects, Painters, and Sculptors*) that the sculptor "brought his figures to actual motion. There is a life-size David, nude and in bronze, so natural in its vivacity and softness that it is almost impossible to believe that it was not molded on the living form." [36]

Artistic Perspective

The first of the great naturalistic painters after Giotto was the Italian painter Tommaso di Giovanni di Simone Guidi, born in 1401 and better known as Masaccio or Sloppy Tom because of his untidy appearance. Masaccio's paintings in Pisa and Florentine churches in the late 1420s served as the models for much of the later Renaissance art.

To the realistic detail found in Giotto's work, Masaccio added a three-dimensional quality. A Masaccio painting looks like it has depth, with objects and people in the foreground appearing closer and more detailed than those in the background. This three-dimensional effect is known as perspective, and as Leonardo da Vinci would later explain it, "there is no object so large but that at great distance from the eye it does not appear smaller than a smaller object near. Among objects of equal size, that which is most remote from the eye will look the smallest."[37]

Masaccio learned perspective from a Florentine architect and painter named Filippo Brunelleschi. Brunelleschi in turn became interested in perspective while preparing architectural drawings of buildings. Determined to learn more, the Florentine first read about the subject in a classical book, the *Ten Books on Architecture* by the first-century B.C. Roman Vitruvius. Brunelleschi then studied geometry, after which he was able to work out the mathematical principles of perspective.

Oil Paints

Another important breakthrough in Renaissance painting was the development of oil paints, whose use was pioneered by early-fifteenth-century Dutch painters such as Jan and Hubert van Eyck. Prior to oil paints, European artists used the media of fresco or tempera. With fresco, an artist applied paint pigment to the wet plaster of a wall and had to work quickly in order to finish before the plaster dried. Tempera, a mixture of paint pigments, egg yolks, and water, allowed the artist more time, but colors tended to look muddy.

Oil paints, on the other hand, which are mixtures of paint pigments and linseed oil, gave artists a number of advantages over both fresco and tempera. First, oils dried slowly so that an artist's pace could be slower. Second, clearer colors with more shades were possible using oils, and the vividness of these colors was easily heightened by coating the painting with varnish. Robert Ergang points out that artists working with oil paints achieved "a workmanship and beauty of color that had been impossible with the use of tempera [and fresco]."[38]

Leonardo da Vinci

All of this thirteenth- and fourteenth-century experimentation and development laid the foundation in Italy for a great burst of artistic activity known as the High Renaissance. This brief period, which covered the last decades of the fifteenth century and the first few of the sixteenth, included works by many of the greatest Renaissance artists, among whom was Leonardo da Vinci.

For a man who listed his profession as painter, Leonardo da Vinci, born in 1452, left behind a mere handful of paintings. But then Leonardo, far more than just a painter, was also an engineer, mathematician, inventor, architect, and writer. Moreover, he was a scientist whose interest in biology, physics, and chemistry is recorded in his 120 notebooks. He was even an accomplished musician, playing a stringed instrument called the lute.

None of these other interests kept Leonardo from creating painted masterpieces. Indeed, the aim of his studies, particularly those in anatomy, was to improve his paintings. He believed firmly that studying the paintings of others alone would produce only minor work. However, a painter who also studied nature would, in his opinion, produce great art.

Leonardo further felt that an artist should not just paint the outer person but, as he wrote, strive to capture "the intention of the soul."[39] Thus, he took painstaking care to reveal through physical detail the character and personality of his subjects, following the advice of Alberti that a painting "will move spectators when the men painted in the picture outwardly demonstrate their own feelings as clearly as possible."[40] In *The Last Supper* (1498), for instance, unlike other Renaissance artists, Leonardo did not physically isolate Judas to reveal the latter's guilt. Instead, Judas is one among the other disciples. His coming betrayal of Christ is revealed through the expression on his face and the posture of his body. The faces and bodies of the other disciples also display their emotions, ranging from horror to sadness to anger to curiosity.

Michelangelo

Somewhat younger than Leonardo was the second of the great High Renaissance artists, Michelangelo Buonarroti, who was born in 1475. Like Leonardo, Michelangelo's interests were varied, but unlike the former, he put most of his

Training the Young Painter

In The Notebooks of Leonardo da Vinci *is found the following advice to young artists.*

The youth should first learn perspective, then the proportions of objects. Then he may copy from some good master, to accustom himself with fine forms. Then [copy] from nature, to confirm by practice the rules he has learned. Then see for a time the works of various masters. Then get the habit of putting his art into practice and work.

It is indispensable to a Painter who would be thoroughly familiar with the limbs in all the position and actions of which they are capable, in the nude, to know the anatomy of the sinews, bones, muscles, and tendons.

The mind of the painter must resemble a mirror, which always takes the color of the object it reflects and is completely occupied by the images of as many objects as are in front of it. You cannot be a good one if you are not the universal master of representing by your art every kind of form produced by nature. And this you will not know how to do if you do not see them, and retain them in your mind.

Leonardo da Vinci, *The Notebooks of Leonardo da Vinci: A New Selection.* Ed. Pamela Taylor. Trans. Jean Paul Richter. New York: New American Library, 1960.

Michelangelo's **Pietà** *is a masterly example of Renaissance sculpture: natural, lifelike figures that seem about to move.*

energies into his art, both sculpting and painting.

Michelangelo was a master of perspective, anatomy, and motion, as can be seen in his greatest painted work, the ceiling of the Sistine Chapel at the Vatican in Rome. In four years, from 1508 to 1512, he singlehandedly painted close to 350 figures, all engaged in major scenes from the book of Genesis. Michelangelo painted the figures, all anatomically correct nudes, in a range of postures and with faces displaying a variety of emotions.

The same sort of naturalism marks Michelangelo's sculpture. However, he was not necessarily concerned with being literally realistic. In his statue of Moses, for example, the face of the prophet is divided, one half showing compassion, the other, sternness. In the 1498 *Pietà*, which shows a grieving Mary holding the body of Christ, the mother's face is younger than the son's because, as Michelangelo once explained, "a woman of perfect purity would keep her youth forever."[41]

Northern Europe and Albrecht Dürer

At the same time that Leonardo, Michelangelo, and other High Renaissance artists were painting and sculpting in Italy, northern European artists were also doing noteworthy work. In Germany, the painter and engraver Albrecht Dürer, born in 1471 and often called "the Leonardo of Germany" because of the broad range of his interests, advanced the study of perspective and human anatomy. Toward the end of his life Dürer wrote several studies on these two subjects.

His most important contribution, however, was not in painting but in engraving. Dürer developed several new techniques that improved the quality of copper engravings and woodcuts. Using Dürer's techniques, printers were able to make reliable reproductions of drawings for books.

Hans Holbein the Younger

Another major northern European artist was the sixteenth-century German painter Hans Holbein. Known as "the Younger"

Perhaps the most famous portrait of England's Henry VIII is this one by German master Hans Holbein.

to distinguish him from his artist father, Holbein spent time in Italy, where he learned composition and perspective, and then in Switzerland, where he met Erasmus, for whom he illustrated *Praise of Folly*. In 1526 the German artist moved to England, where he spent most of the rest of his life.

In England Holbein became friends with Sir Thomas More, for whom he painted two portraits, one of the English humanist and another of the whole More family. These were the first of many Holbein portraits of Renaissance notables, and it was as a portrait painter that the German became famous. Among Holbein's best-known works were paintings of Erasmus in his study and of Henry VIII, for whom Holbein was court painter.

Pieter Brueghel and Everyday Life

Germany was not the only source of northern European artists. From the Netherlands came Pieter Brueghel, born in 1525. Brueghel was one of the first Renaissance artists to paint scenes from everyday life. Later northern European painters, including Brueghel's sons, also became interested in the subject, one that

Dutch master Pieter Brueghel preferred to paint scenes from everyday life, such as this depiction of a peasant wedding in 1568.

held little interest for Italian artists. Describing these northern artists, Ergang observes:

> What the painter portrayed was the commonplace, the natural, or something close to nature. The subjects, whether a beggar, children at play, or an old woman threading a needle, were portrayed by the painters with the zest of a Michelangelo. The artists bestowed on their paintings all the grace and skill they could muster, thereby contributing much to the ennoblement of mundane life. [42]

Brueghel himself was very interested in peasant life and visited villages, observing and sketching, as well as occasionally joining in village activities. Later, he turned his sketches into paintings of peasant weddings, festivals, and dances. He also did a number of landscapes, detailing the cycle of farm life during the year from plowing to planting to harvesting.

Music

In addition to the visual arts, experimentation was just as common in Renaissance music. Innovation saw the creation of new, more complex forms of music, emerging in France, Belgium, and the Netherlands at the very beginning of the Renaissance. These compositions generally had two or more melodies played simultaneously and woven into a harmonic whole. The interweaving of melodies is known as counterpoint. To play this music, new instruments were invented, among them the violin and the harpsichord.

Italian Renaissance composer Giovanni Pierluigi da Palestrina was one of the most celebrated of the period.

As did visual artists, musicians found patrons among the powerful and wealthy. Also, as with painting and sculpture, music became more secular, although religious work was still very important, much of it being played during church services in the forms of hymns and masses. However, even the religious compositions had secular elements as many of them were based on popular folk tunes.

One of the most famous composers of the Renaissance was the sixteenth-century Italian Giovanni Pierluigi da Palestrina, who wrote more than five hundred pieces, most of them church music. Known as "the Prince of Music," Palestrina was much admired and imitated, his work becoming models for future music students. Palestrina's compositions became increasingly complex and helped pave the way for Baroque music, which dominated the seventeenth century.

An Italian contemporary of Palestrina was Vincenzo Galilei, father of the famous scientist Galileo Galilei. Although a composer of songs and other music, Galilei was best known for his writings on music theory. In his musical studies he argued against the Renaissance custom of having a number of singers vocalize simultaneously. Galilei pointed out that this style of singing made it difficult to understand the words. Instead, he championed solo singing, a practice that became more common toward the end of the Renaissance and led eventually in the next century to the development of opera with its emphasis on one singer vocalizing at a time.

Innovation and invention were also characteristic of Renaissance literature. In poetry, prose, and drama European writers created new forms and produced lasting classics that continue to influence writers to this very day.

Chapter Six

The Literary World

Beginning with the Italian poet Dante Alighieri and ending with the English playwright William Shakespeare, innovation was the hallmark of Renaissance literature. Renaissance writers, many of them writing in their native languages rather than the traditional Latin, introduced new forms, such as the sonnet and the novel, and found their themes in the secular world around them.

The Vernacular

As in art, humanism influenced Renaissance literature through both its ideas and its focus on classical myths and ancient writings, around which poetry and prose could be molded. Yet one of the most important developments in Renaissance literature did not come from the humanists: the expanded use in books and poems of such languages as Italian, French, and English rather than Latin. Although Latin remained the inter-national language of Europe and was spoken and written by all university-educated people, Renaissance authors increasingly wrote in their native languages. Such local or regional language was known as vernacular.

The feelings of humanists toward the rise of the vernacular were mixed. Some felt that only Latin was appropriate for literature. Others, such as Petrarch, saw the use of the vernacular as a means of passing on classical virtues and knowledge to a far wider audience than was possible with Latin. And, indeed, members of the rising middle class were more likely to be able to read and write in their own language than in Latin. Scholars Thomas G. Bergin and Jennifer Speake note that Petrarch's "determination that the classical ideal should permeate every aspect of life led to what has been called the 'humanism of the vernacular': the ennobling not only of the native tongue, but also of everyday

This illustration depicts the theme of the Renaissance poem The Fight Between Virtue and Fortune, *which was written in French, the poet's vernacular.*

experience under the influence of classical models."[43]

Poets and other writers were generally enthusiastic about the use of the vernacular, feeling that their native languages brought their work alive in a way no ancient language could. In his 1549 *La Defénse et illustration de la langue française* (*The Defense and Illustration of the French Language*), the French poet Joachim du Bellay writes:

> I cannot wonder at the strange opinion of certain scholars, who think our native language is useless for literature and scholarship. The time will come perhaps when our language, which is already throwing out roots, will rise from the earth and grow great enough to equal the Greeks and Romans themselves, producing like them Homers, Virgils, and Ciceros.[44]

Dante and the Vernacular

The first great vernacular writer was the Italian poet Dante Alighieri. Born in Florence in 1265, Dante was active in public affairs until 1302, when his political party fell out of favor and he was exiled from the city. He spent the next twenty years roaming Italy until his death in 1321.

With little else to do, Dante, who had composed some poetry before his exile, turned his full attention to writing. Among his works during this period was the *De vulgari eloquentia* (*On Elegance in the Vernacular Tongue*, ca. 1304), in which he forcibly argues that Italian is a suitable language for literature.

In keeping with his position in *De vulgari*, Dante's own *Vita nuova* (*New Life*, 1300) was a collection of poems written in Italian. Finished two years before his banishment from Florence, these poems celebrate Dante's love for Beatrice, whom he had first met when they were both children. In the poems, however, Beatrice is not a real person but rather a symbol for an idealized, nonphysical love.

Poet Dante Alighieri holds his vernacular masterpiece The Divine Comedy *before an image of the seven-leveled heaven of the poem.*

Dante also wrote his masterpiece, the *Divina commedia* (*Divine Comedy*), in Italian. Begun around 1307, this lengthy poem was the first major western European work to be written in the vernacular. Divided into three sections, the *Commedia* is Dante's imaginary tour of hell, purgatory, and heaven. His guide through the nine circles of hell and along the nine ledges of purgatory is the Roman poet Virgil. However, as a pagan, Virgil cannot enter heaven, and so Dante finishes his tour in the company of Beatrice, who now represents not only love but also spiritual enlightenment.

Petrarch and the Sonnet

Following Dante, the next important experimenter in vernacular writing was Petrarch. Although much of Petrarch's work was in Latin, he wrote a famous sequence of 366 love poems in Italian. Petrarch began writing these poems around 1330, finally assembling them as the *Canzoniere* (*Songbook,* ca. 1349). The whole sequence deals with Petrarch's love for Laura, a married woman whom he first met in 1327 and for whom he had a lifelong, apparently chaste, attachment.

Each of the poems dealing with Laura in the *Canzoniere* is a sonnet, whose name comes from Italian for "little song." All sonnets have fourteen lines, but some, like Petrarch's, are divided into two sections, the first having eight lines, the second, six. A second sonnet form, developed in England and known as Shakespearean, has three sections of four lines each, followed by a two-line conclusion.

Petrarch did not invent the sonnet, which went back a century before his birth. In Dante's *Vita nuova,* for instance, a number of the poems to Beatrice are sonnets. However, whereas Dante wrote about idealized love, Petrarch wrote about real longing and desire, which made his sonnets more forceful and appealing. Robert Ergang observes:

> In his sonnets, Petrarch humanized the love theme and brought it down to earth. Whereas Dante's Beatrice is the allegorical incarnation of theology, Petrarch's Laura is a real flesh and blood woman. She is not an ideal figure like Beatrice. . . . It is her body as a human body that excites Petrarch's imagination. His inspiration is a feeling for lovely form, for lovely nature, for a lovely woman. Although Petrarch spoke of Laura's inner nature only in vague generalities, he carefully recorded every detail of her physical appearance. [45]

The charm of Petrarch's sonnets made them favorites of many readers, with the form becoming so popular that all Renaissance poets after Petrarch felt compelled to write at least one sonnet cycle, sometimes more. Shakespeare even thought that he would be remembered for his sonnets rather than his plays. Even the Florentine ruler Lorenzo de' Medici "attempted that style that excels all other styles." [46] The sonnet's popularity proved enduring, and it long outlived the Renaissance, remaining an admired verse form for more than five hundred years.

A nineteenth-century painting depicts the seventh day of Renaissance writer Boccaccio's Decameron, *the first major work of prose fiction written in the vernacular.*

Boccaccio and Prose Fiction

The third great vernacular writer of Renaissance Italy was Giovanni Boccaccio. Born in 1313, Boccaccio was a contemporary of Petrarch and, like Dante, a Florentine. Sent by his father to Naples to learn business, the fifteen-year-old Boccaccio instead fell in with the humanists of the city and began to write. Between then and his death in 1375, he produced many books as well as works of poetry. Among the books was the first biography of Dante.

Boccaccio's most famous writing is the *Decameron,* which he wrote between 1348 and 1353. This collection of one hundred stories was the first major work of prose fiction in the vernacular. Indeed, it was the first major prose fiction in any European language, ancient or modern, except for a first-century A.D. Roman work called the *Satyricon.* Up to this time nonfiction, particularly theological and philosophical, was the only acceptable prose writing. Europeans considered prose fiction a vulgar and crude form of writing, lacking the complex art of verse. Boccaccio altered these notions because his prose was elegant and his treatment of theme and character sophisticated.

The *Decameron* tells of a group of ten young men and women who spend ten days in the countryside outside Florence while the city is ravaged by plague. On each day each of the ten tells a story, with the tales ranging from the highly religious to the erotic. In general, entertainment was Boccaccio's goal in the *Decameron*. Ernst Breisach writes:

> In well-polished prose Boccaccio lays out a panorama of Renaissance society and since he intended to entertain those features prevail which do that best: wayward monks, greedy priests, domineering and tricky women, young lovers, unfaithful wives, and completely pure heroes

and heroines. On occasion a more serious tale pleads a case, such as religious tolerance.[47]

The *Decameron* proved to be immensely popular, with readers being delighted by the zest and vigor of the storytelling. Additionally, being in prose, it appealed to the growing middle-class readership, who found it easier to read than poetry, which the middle class often found too mannered and obscure.

Rabelais and the Novel

Writing in the vernacular spread quickly beyond Italy. In France the great pio-

Gargantua's Childhood

The following selection shows the often coarse and broad humor of François Rabelais that was one of his charms for Renaissance readers.

Gargantua, from the age of three to five, spent his time like the little children in the country, namely, in drinking, eating, and sleeping; in eating, sleeping, and drinking; in sleeping, drinking, and eating.

He wallowed in the mud, smudged his nose, dirtied his face, ran his shoes over at the heels, and frequently caught flies with his mouth. He wiped his nose on his sleeve and dropped snot in his soup. He sharpened his teeth on a top, washed his hands in his porridge, and combed his hair with a cup. He would set his butt on the ground between two chairs and cover his head with a wet sack. He struck when the iron was cold, put the cart in front of the oxen, reached for too much and got too little, beat the bush without getting the birdie, and always looked a gift horse in the mouth. His father's pups ate from his plate, and he ate from the plate with them. He bit their ears, they scratched his nose, and they licked his chops.

François Rabelais, *The Portable Rabelais.* Ed. and trans. Samuel Putnam. New York: Viking, 1946.

neer in vernacular literature was the French humanist François Rabelais. Born around 1483, Rabelais as a young man became a monk. In 1524 he found himself in trouble with his superiors for studying Greek, which eventually led to his return to the secular world, where he took up medicine.

Around 1530 Rabelais began to write. He not only experimented with writing in French, but he also tried his hand at a new form of prose. The result was the birth of the French novel in a series of books about the giant Gargantua and his son Pantagruel. The first of four novels about the pair, *Le Grandes et Inestimables Chroniques du grand et énorme géant Gargantua* (*The Great and Inestimable Chronicles of the Great and Enormous Giant Gargantua*), appeared in 1532.

Rabelais's Gargantua and Pantagruel books are satires, whose broad humor is often spiced with playful accounts of the characters' eating, drinking, and lovemaking. Although the books poke fun at all aspects of French and European society, their chief targets are the church and medieval ways of thought, to which many northern European schools still clung. Rabelais's attacks on the old French university, the Sorbonne, led to his having to leave Paris for a time, but in general, the novels were popular and well received.

Cervantes and *Don Quixote*

Another important vernacular Renaissance novelist was the Spanish writer Miguel de Cervantes Saavedra, who was born in 1547. Cervantes's life until his late fifties was one of poverty and misfortune. With little formal education, the young Cervantes sought his fortune by joining the Spanish army. During this military service, he was wounded in battle, losing the use of his left hand. Later, on his way home to Spain, he was captured by Ottoman Turks and was imprisoned for five years.

After his release and return to Spain, Cervantes began writing plays and stories, hoping to make a living. Although his plays had some success, in general, he barely scraped by. Indeed, at least twice in his life, the struggling author went to jail because he could not pay his debts.

Cervantes's fortune changed in 1605 with the publication of the first part of his novel *Don Quixote*. Tremendously popular then and now, this novel presents the humorous adventures of Don Quixote, an old Spanish aristocrat who thinks that he is a medieval knight. His delusion leads him into all sorts of trouble, as he battles windmills that he believes are giants and tries to save a peasant girl who he is convinced is a princess.

Accompanying Don Quixote on his travels is another Spanish peasant, Sancho Panza, whose realistic view of life Cervantes contrasts amusingly with the old knight's unworkable idealism. By the end of part two of the novel, published in 1615, the year before Cervantes's death, Don Quixote and Sancho Panza have encountered a large cast of characters and have stumbled through many adventures, all of which spotlight the ills of Spanish and Renaissance society.

Pirating *Don Quixote*

The novel Don Quixote *was so popular and its sale so profitable that many illegal editions were published. In the following 1605 letter, Cervantes authorizes legal action against those responsible for the pirated editions.*

Our lord king has given and granted his privilege and license, duly transmitted that I or anyone whom I empower to do so may print and sell the work in the Kingdoms of Castile and Portugal for a period of ten years, forbidding under penalty that any other individual without my authorization or permission may print or sell it. It has come to my notice that a few persons in the monarchy of Portugal have printed or intend to print the aforesaid book without my authorization or permission. I am conferring all my full and free power on Francisco de Robles, royal bookseller, the lawyer Diego de Alfaya, and Francisco de Mar, each singly or as a group, to initiate criminal action in the proper way and form against the person or persons who have, without my permission, printed the aforesaid book in any region of the Kingdoms of Castile or Portugal. Let them seek punishment and sentencing of those persons under the royal law.

Robert J. Clements and Lorna Levant, eds. and trans., *Renaissance Letters: Revelations of a World Reborn.* New York: New York University Press, 1976.

Cervantes' tale of Don Quixote and Sancho Panza was so popular it was often pirated.

Lope de Vega: Man of Fifteen Hundred Plays

Working at the same time as Cervantes was another important Spanish vernacular writer, Lope Félix de Vega Carpio, born in 1562. Lope de Vega wrote poems, novels, and plays. His poetry ran the range from Petrarchian love sonnets to historical epics. Around 1590 he wrote his first novel, *La Arcadia*, which deals with the joys of country life.

But it was as a playwright that Lope de Vega was most famous. His contemporaries reported that he wrote around fifteen hundred plays, of which some five hundred survive today. Although Lope de Vega favored comedies, he also wrote serious dramas. He took the plots for his plays from all sorts of sources, among which were Spanish history, folk tales and legends, ancient myths, and the Bible. His characters are not particularly realistic, although their speech is correct as to their social position.

The Elizabethan Stage

In England, meanwhile, playwrights were creating many of the major vernacular dramas of the Renaissance. The English theater of the reign of Elizabeth I (1588–1603), called by later historians the Elizabethan Age, was popular with all social classes. These appreciative Elizabethan audiences were entertained by the works of a large number of dramatists, of whom the two greatest were Christopher Marlowe and William Shakespeare.

Christopher Marlowe, born in 1564, is something of a mystery man. A graduate of Cambridge University, he appears to have been a government spy, even while still in school. He reportedly traveled to other countries on secret missions, the details of which are lost. His death is just as shrouded in mystery as his spying activities. He died young, at the age of twenty-nine, supposedly killed in a brawl over a tavern bill. Yet to this day, rumors circulate that he was assassinated.

No matter the truth about his death, in his short life span Marlowe wrote half a dozen of the most popular plays of the Elizabethan period. Some, such as the two parts of *Tamburlaine the Great* (1587) and *The Troublesome Reign and Lamentable Death of Edward II, King of England* (1594), are grand, sweeping historical

A woodcut portrays a scene from Christopher Marlowe's play The Famous Tragedy of the Rich Jew of Malta.

William Shakespeare emerged as the brightest play-writing star of his day. This scene is from Othello, the Moor of Venice, *one of his great tragedies.*

sagas. Others, like *The Tragic History of Dr. Faustus* (ca. 1589) and *The Famous Tragedy of the Rich Jew of Malta* (ca. 1590), are tragedies, in which personal flaws bring down the lead characters.

A number of factors made Marlowe's plays so popular with the Elizabethans. First, he wrote using vivid and forceful language. Second, he populated the stage with dynamic characters, who develop and change during the course of the play. Third, he researched his plays to make them more realistic. Finally, he added large doses of intrigue, action, and violence.

The Great Dramatist

Marlowe was not the only playwright of his day who knew how to use language to develop characters and to drive plots with action and violence. Indeed, he had

parts of *Henry VI*. He quickly followed with a series of history plays, comedies, and tragedies, which included *Richard III* (ca. 1592), *The Taming of the Shrew* (ca. 1594), and *Romeo and Juliet* (ca. 1595). Beginning in 1600, at the height of both his popularity and his creativity, Shakespeare wrote his four great tragedies, *Hamlet* (ca. 1600), *Othello* (ca. 1605), *King Lear* (ca. 1605), and *Macbeth* (ca. 1606). He died in 1616, and seven years later his friends published the first collection of his plays, known as the First Folio.

Shakespeare's dramas were even more popular than Marlowe's, and his success made him rich within a decade of his arrival in London. Audiences enjoyed his clever and imaginative use of English, his vivid characters, and his elaborate plots, which in the later plays hinge upon the personalities of his characters. An added appeal, as Emil Lucki points out, is the plays' "breadth of spirit. The idea that life is great and meaningful and enjoyable appears constantly; and the fact that the message is conveyed more by implication or suggestion than by open declaration heightens its appeal."[48]

It is these elements that have made Shakespeare the most famous writer in English literature. Even today, four hundred years after his death, his plays are read and seen by more people all over the world than the dramas of any other playwright living or dead. His plays have served as the basis for other plays, operas, and movies. Fellow Elizabethan dramatist Ben Jonson observed in the First Folio that "he was not of an age, but for all time."[49]

any number of competitors, one of whom, William Shakespeare, would surpass him in both ability and fame.

Shakespeare, born in Stratford-upon-Avon in 1564, arrived in London sometime in the late 1580s. There, he eventually joined one of the city's leading theater companies, Lord Chamberlain's Men, later known as the King's Men. Shakespeare did some acting with the troupe, but his primary duty was to write plays, which he began doing around 1589 with the three

Elizabethan Poets and Essayists

In addition to playwrights, the Elizabethans also produced a number of other accomplished writers. It was an age of poets. Some, such as the explorer and politician Sir Walter Raleigh, merely dabbled in verse. Others, however, took poetry more seriously.

Among these latter was Edmund Spenser, born in about 1552. Spenser's major work was the *Faerie Queene,* begun around 1580 and left unfinished upon the poet's death in 1599. This long poem, written in a very difficult rhyme scheme that now bears Spenser's name, is set in a medieval kingdom meant to represent Elizabethan England. Spenser loaded the poem with a host of references to then-current religious and political issues.

Prose writers also flourished during the Elizabethan period, one of the most accomplished being Sir Francis Bacon, born in 1561. Beginning in 1597, Bacon wrote a series of essays in which he reflected upon such topics as truth, death, atheism, and marriage. However, his most important writing dealt with the newly emerging experimental science of the Renaissance. One of the most important legacies of the period, European science would become, as Charles G. Nauert points out, "the most exportable Western commodity, for the science of the West has penetrated and transformed even resolutely anti-Western civilizations that have easily resisted the influence of Western religion, Western philosophy, and Western artistic and literary traditions." [50]

Chapter Seven

Scientists and Physicians

The intellectual energies of the Renaissance went not only into art, music, and literature but also into science and medicine. Influenced by humanism, Renaissance Europeans began a systematic study of nature. These investigations led to discoveries, particularly in astronomy, physics, and medicine, that increased human understanding of the natural world.

The Beginnings of Science

Vital to the growth of scientific investigation was a gradual rejection of astrology and magic, belief in which was common during the Middle Ages. Sir Francis Bacon warned in his 1620 *Novum organum* (*New Organ*) that these superstitions were harmful to the pursuit of science, which Renaissance scholars frequently called natural philosophy: "The corruption of philosophy by superstition is most injurious to it both as a whole and in parts." Later, he added that "there is much difference in philosophy between their [superstitions'] absurdity and real science."[51] In general, the scientists of the day rejected any sort of magic because it was not supported by observation and experimentation, although a few astronomers, such as the sixteenth-century Dane Tycho Brahe, continued to believe that the stars did affect human destiny.

Important also to the development of science was humanism, for among the ancient writings that the humanists collected were those that inspired scientific research. As the Polish astronomer Nicolaus Copernicus wrote in 1543, "I took the trouble to reread all the books by [ancient] philosophers which I could get hold of."[52] Impressed after reading the studies of such ancient Greeks as Archimedes and Hero of Alexandria, some Renaissance scholars decided to try their own hand at teasing out the secrets of nature.

A sixteenth-century painting shows astronomers observing an eclipse of the sun. The period saw a rebirth of scientific inquiry as well as of art and commerce.

Numbers and Symbols

Renaissance scientists further discovered in these ancient texts a powerful tool, mathematics. Renaissance philosophers began using mathematics to discover the relationships between observed events, and it was during the Renaissance that math and science became closely linked. Indeed, many of the great scientists of the day, such as Galileo, trained first as mathematicians. According to historians Stephen Toulmin and June Goodfield, the idea "grew up that *mathematical axioms* were the true principles of things. In order to explain why things are as they are and behave as they do, things must conform to certain mathematical equations."[53]

Beginning with the mathematics inherited from the ancient Greeks and Romans, Renaissance thinkers undertook their own mathematical explorations. Among Renaissance math inventions was the decimal, introduced in 1586 by Belgian mathematician Simon Stevin. Decimals are a different way of writing fractions, making it easier to add, subtract, multiply, and divide them. Their use immensely simplifies complex calculations.

A few years later, in France, François Viète proposed in his 1591 book *In artem analyticam isagoge* (*Introduction to the Analytical Arts*) that letters, such as *x, y,* and *z,* be substituted in algebraic formulas for known and unknown quantities, which up to then had often been written out as full words and phrases. Viète's proposal created a flexible mathematical language that made such higher math as calculus possible.

Critics of Research

The humanists might have supplied the classical texts to Renaissance scientists and mathematicians, but many rejected research because they firmly believed that everything that could be known was already included in the books of antiquity. These critics of new research also thought that the old Greek and Roman writers could never be wrong in any of their facts or conclusions. Scholar Anthony Grafton writes:

The humanists had failed to see that the world had changed that modern technology was more powerful than those of the ancients. They had confused the fact that their texts had existed for a long time with the authority that human beings gain as they age—an authority that can only be invested in people who continue to learn as they age, not in books, which are impervious to experience.[54]

Leonardo da Vinci, for instance, genius though he was, could not shake off this acceptance of classical authority while studying the way blood moved through the human heart. The ancient expert on these matters was the second-century A.D.

An insatiable scientific curiosity drove Leonardo da Vinci to render many drawings of human anatomy such as this.

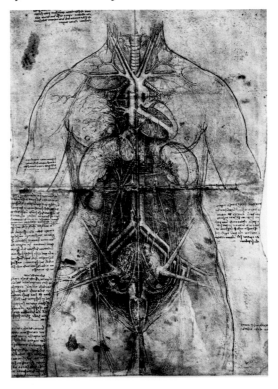

Greek physician Galen, who claimed that clearly visible pores let blood flow from one chamber of the heart to another. Such pores do not exist. But when Leonardo could not find these pores, he decided that he, not Galen, was mistaken.

The Scientific Theory

However, Leonardo did not always give way to ancient authority. His studies of the geology of the Po River valley convinced him that the entire area was at least two hundred thousand years old, making Earth far older than classical authorities claimed.

Leonardo, in his haphazard way, as well as other Renaissance scientists in more determined fashion, showed the importance of observation, particularly when linked to experimentation, for any type of research. Up to this time, most philosophers followed the common practice in ancient Greece and Rome of using logic alone to get at the laws of nature. These logic-produced theories were tested only with more logic rather than by devising an experiment to show whether they worked in the real world.

In 1605 Sir Francis Bacon argued in his *Advancement of Learning* that logic must be supported with information gained from experiments in order for any theory to be judged correct. Then, the conclusion drawn from this information must be tested with further experiments. Bacon's scientific method underlies all scientific research down to the present day. Charles G. Nauert points out:

Bacon saw that the new "natural philosophy" (or "science" as we would call it) would have to be experimental and that scientific conclusions would have to be demonstrated theories. . . . Bacon realized that the logic of science would have to direct the mind in processing from observed phenomena (experimental data) to broad generalizations.[55]

The Moving Earth

Bacon did not invent the scientific method; it had already been in use for some time. Indeed, it lay at the heart of the scientific work of Polish astronomer Nicolaus Copernicus. Born in 1473 and educated at universities in both Poland and Italy, Copernicus forever changed the way Western civilization looks at the universe and in the process launched modern astronomy. At the time of Copernicus's birth, Europeans believed that Earth sat stationary at the center of the universe. All other heavenly bodies, including the Sun, supposedly revolved around Earth. This belief had been passed to the Renaissance in the writings of classical astronomers.

However, Copernicus used observation and mathematical analysis to overturn this concept. With instruments he built himself, the astronomer studied the night sky for years, while taking careful notes. Calculations using this collected information showed him that it was Earth, not the Sun, that moves. Copernicus realized that Earth both revolves around the Sun and rotates about its own axis. The Polish scientist eventually published his findings in the 1543 *De revolu-*

Judging Copernicus

In his introduction to Nicolaus Copernicus's On the Revolutions of Heavenly Spheres *(1543), the Protestant clergyman Andrew Osiander asks readers to keep an open mind about the proposal that Earth orbits the Sun and not the reverse.*

Since the newness of the hypothesis of this work—which sets the earth in motion and puts an immovable sun at the center of the universe—has already received a great deal of publicity, I have no doubt that certain of the philosophers have taken grave offense and think it wrong to raise any disturbance among disciplines which have had the right set-up for a long time now. If, however, they are willing to weigh the matter scrupulously, they will find that the author of this work has done nothing which merits blame. For it is the job of the astronomer to use painstaking and skilled observation in gathering together the history of the celestial movements and then to think up or construct whatever causes or hypotheses he pleases such that, by the assumption of these causes, these same movements can be calculated from the principles of geometry.

Nicolaus Copernicus, *On the Revolutions of Heavenly Spheres.* Trans. Charles Glenn Wallis. Chicago: Encyclopaedia Britannica, 1939.

---

tionibus orbium coelestium (*On the Revolutions of Heavenly Spheres*).

The Reaction to Copernicus

Copernicus's theory, known as Copernicanism, met with a mixture of disbelief and hostility since it contradicted classical astronomy. Indeed, the Polish astronomer had finished *De revolutionibus* thirteen years before its publication but had initially decided not to publish it because he had feared the reaction of critics. In fact, he almost abandoned the whole project, writing that "the scorn which I had to fear on account of the newness and absurdity of my opinion almost drove me to abandon a work already undertaken."[56]

In addition to contradicting the ancients, Copernicanism aroused hostility for another important reason. His theory was seen as a threat to humanity's place in the cosmos. While Earth was the center of the universe, so were humans and their concerns. But with Earth shifted from that center, so were people, and their cosmic importance, as well as their relationship to the universe, became less certain. Many philosophers, particularly theologians, bitterly resented and resisted this lessening of human significance.

Falling Bodies

Not all Renaissance scholars and philosophers rejected Copernicus's ideas. One of Copernicus's most enthusiastic supporters was Galileo Galilei, born in 1564 in Pisa, Italy. Initially, Galileo's scientific interest was in physics, specifically the study of falling objects. In his 1591 book *De motu* (*On Motion*), he describes a series of experiments that show, among other things, that both light and heavy bodies fall at the same rate. Later, he showed that falling objects accelerated at a constant rate. Both of these conclusions brought a storm of criticism from many philosophers because Galileo's claims challenged Aristotle, who had stated just the opposite. Galileo, however, was putting into practice what Sir Francis Bacon would put into words a decade and half later when he argued for "the study of things themselves. Be not forever the property of one man."[57]

Galileo shows his telescope to the duke of Venice in this painting. Galileo's support of Copernicus's theories got him in trouble with church authorities.

The conclusions reached by Copernicus and Galileo were arrived at through painstaking observation, which in Galileo's case often meant experimentation and careful record keeping. For example, the success of Galileo's falling-body studies depended upon reliable records of times and distances. Galileo used the information from these records to work out the mathematical relationships involved in his experiments. Other Renaissance researchers made similar calculations in their work, and in doing so, they helped create modern science.

Opening the Heavens

Studying the heavens, however, in support of Copernicanism was a more difficult task than Galileo's falling-body problems. The human eye could only see so much, and because of this limitation, little evidence existed to support Copernicanism through the end of the sixteenth century. In 1608 matters quickly changed with the invention of the telescope in the Netherlands. Although credit for the invention generally goes to the spectacles maker Hans Lippershey, a number of individuals appear to have arrived at the idea simultaneously.

Galileo was quick to grasp the telescope's importance to astronomical observation and built his own. In late 1609 he turned his new instrument skyward. One of his first discoveries was that the Moon's surface was covered with craters, mountains, and valleys. This observation pleased him, for it destroyed another Aristotelian claim that heavenly bodies were perfect, lacking blemishes or defects.

Galileo's second great discovery pleased him even more and gave him ammunition against critics of Copernicanism. In early 1610 he spotted the four largest moons of Jupiter. Copernicus's critics had wanted to know why an Earth moving around the Sun did not leave the Moon behind. Although Galileo still could not explain why the Moon kept pace with Earth, he now could point to a known moving planet, Jupiter, which carried its orbiting satellites with it. He reasoned that a moving Earth and its Moon should act the same.

Dialogue and Trial

Galileo continued to argue vigorously for Copernicus's ideas, ignoring advice from friends to keep his opinions to himself. His blunt and often insulting comments were making powerful enemies, particularly among the supporters of Aristotle. In 1632 he published his *Dialogo dei due massimi sistemi del mondo* (*Dialogue on the Great World Systems*), which clearly shows his enthusiasm for Copernicanism and his contempt for Aristotelianism. Aristotelians in the church soon convinced Pope Urban VIII that Galileo's attack on Aristotle, whose writings had long since become an important part of church doctrine, was an attack against Catholicism. They emphasized the danger by pointing out that the *Dialogue* was written in Italian, not the usual Latin, and so its potential audience was very large, as was the potential harm to the church.

Persuading Galileo

In a 1633 letter Cardinal Vincenzio da Firenzuola explains how Galileo came to renounce Copernicanism during his heresy trial.

Their Eminences of the Holy Congregation [the Inquisition] took up the case of Galileo, reviewing its state briefly. Having approved what had been done thus far, they then considered various difficulties as to the manner of prosecuting the case, and getting it speedily under way. In particular because Galileo denied in his hearing that which is evident in the book he wrote. I proposed a means: that the Holy Congregation grant me power to deal with Galileo to the end of convincing him of his error, and bringing him to the point when he understood of confessing it. It appeared at first sight too daring a proposal; there seemed little hope of succeeding by means of reasonable persuasion; but they gave me the power. I went to reason with Galileo yesterday, and after many exchanges between us, I gained my point, for I made him see plainly his error, so that he clearly knew that he was in the wrong, and that his book had gone too far. He agreed to confess it.

Robert J. Clements and Lorna Levant, eds. and trans., *Renaissance Letters: Revelations of a World Reborn.* New York: New York University Press, 1976.

The pope had publication of the *Dialogue* stopped within six months of its appearance and had Galileo brought to trial for heresy, at the end of which the scientist publicly abandoned Copernican thought. The alternative was torture and death. Despite his forced denial, Galileo never lost faith in the Copernican system. Other Renaissance astronomers performed observations that would eventually lead to the general acceptance of the moving Earth.

The Church and Science

Although it might seem from the church's treatment of Galileo that it was hostile toward science, such was not the case. Indeed, Copernicus had been a monk, and many of the leading astronomers of the day were Jesuits, such as the German Christoph Scheiner, Galileo's contemporary and the discoverer of sunspots. Urban himself, before becoming pope, had been a leading mathematician.

In general, the church had no quarrel with the scientific findings of the day. It was even willing to accept Copernicanism as a useful tool since it better predicted the movements of the other planets than did older theories. Yet the church felt that to admit that Copernicanism was a true depiction of the universe would be to undermine centuries of church teachings and perhaps the church itself. At a time when Catholicism was locked in battle with Protestantism, any threat was too great to allow to exist. Thus, the church felt it had no choice but to silence those like Galileo who too publicly argued for the moving Earth.

Geology and Biology

Renaissance advances in other sciences were not as dramatic or as sweeping as those coming from astronomy and physics, although another physical science, geology, fared well during the period. Geology was tied to mining, one of the most profitable of Renaissance industries, and its study was encouraged by mine owners. The 1556 mining handbook *De re metallica* (*All About Metals*), written by the German geologist Georgius Agricola, gives very clear and useful descriptions of different kinds of soils and rocks.

The biological sciences, on the other hand, saw only modest progress during the Renaissance. Biology and botany were confined to halfhearted stabs at creating catalogs of animals and plants.

Medical Advances

The related field of medicine, however, made some strides during the Renaissance, although in general doctors still held tightly to ideas proposed by Galen. In part, medical progress was spurred on

Andreas Vesalius teaches an anatomy lesson in this painting. Vesalius's studies in anatomy greatly advanced medical science.

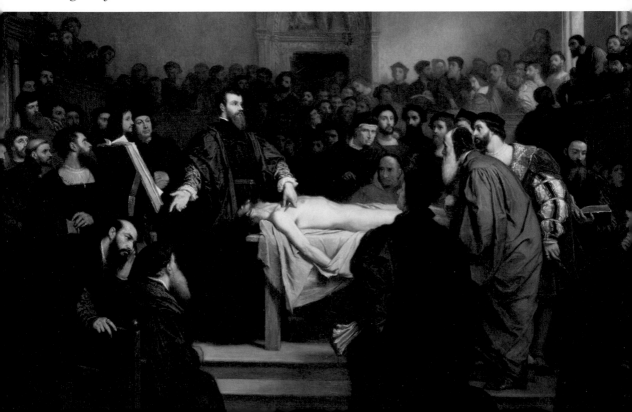

by the appearance in the fourteenth century of the Black Death—a deadly plague that killed as much as a third of Europe's population—and in the fifteenth of syphilis. Neither disease had been known to Galen, and Renaissance doctors thus were forced to experiment if they wanted to find treatments. They were unsuccessful in halting the devastating Black Death, but a German physician, Philippus Aureolus Theophrastus Bombast von Hohenheim, known as Paracelsus, discovered in 1530 that drinking mercury compounds was an effective treatment for syphilis.

The greatest advance in the medicine of the period was an increased understanding of human anatomy, due in large part to the work of Andreas Vesalius. Born in 1514 in Belgium, Vesalius was the son and grandson of doctors. After studying medicine in Paris, he became interested in human anatomy, hoping to improve on the information passed down by Galen. Unlike the ancient Greek, who had depended mostly on the dissection of animals, Vesalius used human bodies whenever possible. By keeping an open mind and possessing a keen eye for detail, the Renaissance anatomist improved on and corrected Galen's work.

In 1543 Vesalius published *De humani corporis fabrica* (*On the Structure of the Human Body*), in which he describes his findings. Accompanying the text were detailed illustrations made from very accurate woodcut diagrams. *De humani* quickly became the standard human anatomy text of its time.

Clocks and Microscopes

Along with an increasing understanding of the natural world during the Renaissance came inventions. As Bacon observed at the time, "We should note the force, effect, and consequences of inventions, which were unknown to the ancients, such as printing. For these have changed the appearance of the whole world."[58]

One of the earliest inventions of the period was the mechanical clock. Introduced in the mid-fourteenth century, such clocks were run first by weights and then by coiled springs. The latter invention led in 1504 to the first pocket watch, made by the German locksmith Peter Henlein. These early mechanical clocks were none too precise, but they eventually led to more exact timepieces, which would prove essential to researchers needing accurate time measurements when running experiments.

Along with the telescope, the most important invention of the period was the compound microscope, which first appeared in 1590. Because it had two lenses, this microscope was a more powerful magnifier than a single-lens magnifying glass. Its inventor may have been Dutch spectacles maker Zacharias Janssen, although many others claimed credit, including the supposed inventor of the telescope, Hans Lippershey. Beginning in the middle of the seventeenth century, this instrument proved to be the first key to unlocking the secrets of the normally invisible microscopic world.

Michelangelo's paintings on the Sistine Chapel ceiling in the Vatican sum up the spirit of the Renaissance's legacy: new yet ancient, spiritual yet very human.

Modern science was only beginning by the end of the Renaissance, yet its form was already visible in Bacon's writings and in the work of Galileo and others. The rationality and reason promoted by Renaissance researchers would become increasingly important not only to science but to all western thought as well. Those who came after this period would refine its methods and techniques and open up much more of the natural world to human understanding, but they would always be indebted to the pioneering work of these early scientific thinkers.

The Birth of the Modern World

Just as the Middle Ages had gradually merged with and become one with the Renaissance, so during the course of the seventeenth century did the Renaissance alter and become the modern age, with the modern growing naturally out of the political, social, economic, artistic, and scientific trends of Renaissance Europe.

Unlike the pre-Renaissance world, the modern one would be an international arena in which European civilization and affairs met and often clashed with cultures in the Americas, Asia, and Africa. It would be a world of strong national states, tied together in tight economic and political nets, and it would be a world built upon scientific principles and technology.

The Renaissance is certainly important for having laid the foundation of the present-day world, and yet, even though it is centuries in the past, this age is more than an interesting antique. In many ways it still lives because of the rich and lasting legacy that it passed down to the current age. As Bergin and Speake write, "For historians the age of the Renaissance had an ending, as all human things must, but in a deeper and truer sense the Renaissance is still alive. The creations of its great artists are still contemplated with awe, its men of letters are still read and indeed are still 'best sellers.'"[59]

Notes

Introduction: Leaving the Middle Ages

1. Charles G. Nauert, *The Age of the Renaissance and Reformation*. Washington, DC: University Press of America, 1977, p. 1.
2. Quoted in Peter Burke, *The Renaissance*. London: Longmans, 1964, p. 6.
3. Quoted in Burke, *The Renaissance*, pp. 21–22.
4. Robert Ergang, *The Renaissance*. Princeton, NJ: Van Nostrand, 1967, p. 1.

Chapter One: The New Learning

5. Crane Brinton, John B. Christopher, and Robert Lee Wolff, *A History of Civilization*, vol. 1, *Prehistory to 1715*, 2nd ed. Englewood Cliffs, NJ: Prentice-Hall, 1960, p. 444.
6. Will Durant, *The Story of Civilization*, vol. 4, *The Age of Faith*. New York: Simon and Schuster, 1950, p. 443.
7. Brinton, *A History of Civilization*, p. 444.
8. Ernst Breisach, *Renaissance Europe: 1300–1517*. New York: Macmillan, 1973, p. 314.
9. Quoted in Brinton, *A History of Civilization*, pp. 422–23.
10. Marsilio Ficino, *The Philebus Commentary*, trans. Michael J.B. Allen. Berkeley and Los Angeles: University of California Press, 1975, p. 78.
11. Quoted in Samuel Dresden, *Humanism in the Renaissance*, trans. Margaret King. New York: McGraw-Hill, 1968, p. 11.
12. John Hale, *The Civilization of Europe in the Renaissance*. New York: Atheneum, 1993, p. 191.

Chapter Two: Religious Reform

13. Quoted in Burke, *The Renaissance*, p. 28.
14. Brinton, *A History of Civilization*, p. 482.
15. Nauert, *The Age of the Renaissance*, p. 119.
16. Will Durant, *The Story of Civilization*, vol. 6, *The Reformation*. New York: Simon and Schuster, 1957, p. 368.
17. Durant, *The Story of Civilization*, vol. 6, p. 895.
18. Hale, *The Civilization of Europe in the Renaissance*, pp. 122–23.

Chapter Three: The Growth of Nations

19. Brinton, *A History of Civilization*, p. 517.
20. Nauert, *The Age of the Renaissance*, pp. 197–98.
21. Niccolò Machiavelli, *The Prince and the Discourses*, trans. Luigi Ricci,

rev. E.R.P. Vincent. New York: Modern Library, 1950, p. 65.

22. Breisach, *Renaissance Europe,* pp. 175–76.
23. Quoted in Donald R. Kelley, *Renaissance Humanism.* Boston: Twayne, 1991, p. 21.
24. Nauert, *The Age of the Renaissance,* p. 97.
25. Breisach, *Renaissance Europe,* p. 138.

Chapter Four: A World of Business

26. Breisach, *Renaissance Europe,* pp. 319–20.
27. Quoted in Hale, *The Civilization of Europe in the Renaissance,* p. 379.
28. Durant, *The Age of Faith,* pp. 619–20.
29. Emil Lucki, *History of the Renaissance: 1350–1550,* vol. 1, *Economy and Society.* Salt Lake City: University of Utah Press, 1963, pp. 46–47.
30. Ergang, *The Renaissance,* p. 80.
31. Will Durant, *The Story of Civilization,* vol. 5, *The Renaissance.* New York: Simon and Schuster, 1953, pp. 70–71.
32. Quoted in Christopher Hibbert, *The Rise and Fall of the House of Medici.* London: Folio Society, 1974, p. 24.
33. Quoted in Hibbert, *The Rise and Fall of the House of Medici,* p. 24.

Chapter Five: Artists and Musicians

34. Breisach, *Renaissance Europe,* pp. 357–58.
35. Leon Battista Alberti, *On Painting,* trans. Cecil Grayson. London: Penguin, 1972, p. 72.
36. Quoted in Burke, *The Renaissance,* p. 45.
37. Leonardo da Vinci, *The Notebooks of Leonardo da Vinci: A New Selection,* ed. Pamela Taylor, and trans. Jean Paul Richter. New York: New American Library, 1960, pp. 32–33.
38. Ergang, *The Renaissance,* p. 390.
39. Quoted in Emil Lucki, *History of the Renaissance: 1350–1550,* vol. 4, *Literature and Art.* Salt Lake City: University of Utah Press, 1965, p. 215.
40. Alberti, *On Painting,* p. 76.
41. Quoted in Lucki, *History of the Renaissance,* vol. 4, p. 169.
42. Ergang, *The Renaissance,* p. 386.

Chapter Six: The Literary World

43. Thomas G. Bergin and Jennifer Speake, eds., *Encyclopedia of the Renaissance.* London: Batsford, 1987, p. 55.
44. Quoted in Burke, *The Renaissance,* pp. 131–32.
45. Ergang, *The Renaissance,* p. 107.
46. Lorenzo de' Medici, *Lorenzo de' Medici: Selected Poems and Prose,* ed. and trans. Jon Thiem. University Park: Pennsylvania State University Press, 1991, p. 113.
47. Breisach, *Renaissance Europe,* pp. 344–45.
48. Lucki, *History of the Renaissance,* vol. 4, p. 111.
49. Quoted in William Shakespeare, *The Complete Works of Shakespeare,* ed. Hardin Craig. Glenview, IL: Scott, Foresman, 1961, p. 48.
50. Nauert, *The Age of the Renaissance,* p. 262.

Chapter Seven: Scientists and Physicians

51. Francis Bacon, *Novum organum.* Chicago: Encyclopaedia Britannica, 1952, pp. 114, 123.

52. Nicolaus Copernicus, *On the Revolutions of Heavenly Spheres,* trans. Charles Glenn Wallis. Chicago: Encyclopaedia Britannica, 1939, p. 508.

53. Stephen Toulmin and June Goodfield, *The Fabric of the Heavens: The Development of Astronomy and Dynamics.* New York: Harper, 1961, p. 70.

54. Quoted in Jill Kraye, ed., *The Cambridge Companion to Renaissance Humanism.* Cambridge, UK: Cambridge University Press, 1996, p. 205.

55. Nauert, *The Age of the Renaissance,* p. 264.

56. Copernicus, *On the Revolutions of Heavenly Spheres,* p. 506.

57. Quoted in Bergin and Speake, eds., *Encyclopedia of the Renaissance,* p. 27.

58. Bacon, *Novum organum,* p. 135.

59. Bergin and Speake, eds., *Encyclopedia of the Renaissance,* p. ix.

Books

James Barter, *Travel Guide to Renaissance Florence.* San Diego: Lucent, 2002. This book, set at the time of Michelangelo, Leonardo da Vinci, and the Medici family, allows readers to experience the sights, sounds, smells, and tastes of Renaissance Florence.

Lucia Corrain, *The Art of the Renaissance.* New York: Bedrick, 2001. This volume provides profiles of many Renaissance artists and explanations of artistic techniques of the period.

Brendan January, *Science in the Renaissance.* Danbury, CT: Watts, 1999. This account details the new approaches and techniques that led to the birth of modern science during the Renaissance.

Stuart Kallen, *A Renaissance Painter's Studio.* San Diego: Lucent, 2002. This volume gives insightful glimpses into the working lives of master painters, revealing how they painted their masterpieces, who paid them, and what life was like working inside their studios.

William W. Lace, *Elizabethan England.* San Diego: Lucent, 2005. Containing excerpts from period documents, a time line, and instructive illustrations, this history covers the reign of Elizabeth I, the height of the English Renaissance.

Don Nardo, *The Trial of Galileo.* San Diego: Lucent, 2004. This account chronicles the events of Galileo's trial for heresy and focuses on its lasting significance. It explains points of church law, introduces important people related to the trial, and discusses interesting and relevant historical information.

Mark R. Nesbitt, ed., *Living in Renaissance Italy.* San Diego: Greenhaven, 2005. This collection of essays, written by both Renaissance writers and modern scholars, covers many topics, such as becoming established in society, the role of art in culture, and the moral code of the era.

Raymond and Loretta Obstfeld, eds., *The Renaissance.* San Diego: Greenhaven, 2002. This anthology gathers primary accounts from religious, artistic, scientific, and secular Renaissance leaders, whose writings cover a broad spectrum of social and political topics of the day.

Virginia Schomp, *The Italian Renaissance.* Tarrytown, NY: Marshall Cavendish, 2003. Color photographs and informative sidebars enliven this history of the birth and development of the Renaissance in Italy.

Melissa Thompson and Ruth Dean, *Women of the Renaissance.* San Diego: Lucent, 2004. This book brings to life the daily work and notable achievements of Renaissance women in their roles as wives and mothers, caregivers, workers, religious leaders, queens, rebels, pirates, scholars, writers and artists.

Web Sites

Art History (http://witcombe.sbc.edu/ ARTHLinks.html). This site, maintained by art historian Christopher L.C.E. Witcombe, contains pages on fifteenth- and sixteenth-century Renaissance art and links to reproductions of works by Leonardo da Vinci, Michelangelo, and a host of other artists of the period.

The Net's Educational Resource Center (http://members.aol.com/teacher net). This useful site contains links to Renaissance overviews, terms, maps, time lines, daily life, culture, and beliefs.

Teacher Oz's Kingdom of History (www.teacheroz.com). This excellent site has many links to Renaissance images and subjects such as art, religion, warfare, and biographies.

Index

Picture Credits

About the Author

James A. Corrick has been a professional writer and editor for twenty-five years. Along with a PhD in English, his academic background includes a graduate degree in the biological sciences. He has taught English, edited magazines for the National Space Society, and edited and indexed books on history, economics, and literature. He and his wife live in Tucson, Arizona. Among his other titles for Lucent are *The Civil War: Life Among the Soldiers and Cavalry, The Louisiana Purchase, Life of a Medieval Knight, The Incas, The Civil War, Life Among the Incas, The Early Middle Ages,* and *The Byzantine Empire.*